P9-CIU-114

THE
250
QUESTIONS
YOU SHOULD ASK TO
GET OUT OF
DEBT

DAVID AND MARCIA RYE

BUSINESS

Avon, Massachusetts

Published by Adams Business
An imprint of Adams Media, a division of F+W Media, Inc.
57 Littlefield Street, Avon, MA 02322. U.S.A.
www.adamsmedia.com

ISBN 10: 1-59869-994-6
ISBN 13: 978-1-59869-994-4

Printed in the United States of America.

J I H G F E D C B A

Library of Congress Cataloging-in-Publication Data
is available from the publisher.

*This book is available at quantity discounts for bulk purchases.
For information, call 1-800-289-0963.*

CONTENTS

Introduction   v

PART 1

Challenging Debt   1

1. Dealing with Your Debt   3
2. Determining Where You Want to Go   10
3. Living on a Budget   17
4. Avoiding Debt Traps   23
5. Checking Your Credit Score   28
6. Consolidating Debts   32
7. Spending Less   37
8. Making Hard Choices   44

PART 2

Finding Money   51

9. Paying Yourself First   53
10. Searching for Hidden Money   57
11. Using Home Equity   63
12. Paying College Expenses   69
13. Controlling Credit Cards   75
14. Avoiding Bad Loans   80
15. Paying Off Debt   86
16. Getting Tax Money Back   90
17. Creating a Savings Plan   97

PART 3

Improving Your Quality of Life   103

18. Acquiring a Car   105
19. Making More Money   113
20. Buying a Home   116
21. Protecting Yourself with Insurance   125
22. Thinking about Retiring   134

PART 4

Putting It All Together   143

23. Assembling Your Financial Plan   145
24. Becoming Financially Independent   151
25. Staying Ahead of the Game   158

Appendix of Resources by Subject   162
The 250 Questions   167
Index   181

WITHDRAWN

INTRODUCTION

Do you ever wake up at night worried about the financial setbacks and conflicts that you're having with your creditors? Do you become aggravated over the fact that you never seem to have enough money to live on? What are you going to do to control the confrontations that erupt when you address the subject with family members? What steps can you take to eliminate the financial mess that you are in?

Unfortunately, tens of millions of Americans are in your shoes. Like you, they are headed for financial disaster if they don't figure out a way to get out of debt.

The 250 Questions You Should Ask to Get Out of Debt has been written to answer your questions. As you read the material in this book, you will quickly learn how to assess the magnitude of your debt problems so that you can determine where you've been, how you got there, and, more important, where you want to go. When you plunge into questions about how to avoid debt traps and how to create a realistic spending plan that works for you, you will discover the answers you've been looking for. You'll find out how you can dramatically improve the overall quality of your life once you eliminate your debt load.

This book contains all of the elements you need to consider to get out of debt and improve your financial well-being. Each chapter includes a set of questions that builds on what you've learned from the previous chapter. Based upon your own situation, select the chapters and questions that cover subjects that are most important to you. That will allow you to maneuver through your personal debt-related issues and make the right decisions to avoid economic catastrophe. The book is filled with real-world examples and supplemented with detailed "here's why it works" illustrations.

Many answers are supplemented with related websites for additional information. As a bonus, you will learn the secrets of becoming financially independent, which are covered in the "Putting It All Together" chapters at the end of the book. The sooner you start mounting an assault on your personal debt, the sooner you will see your debt numbers heading down rather than up. When that happens, you will feel great.

PART 1

Challenging Debt

Chapter 1

DEALING WITH YOUR DEBT

The average debt level of people just like you is a scary 20 percent of their disposable income, not counting their mortgage debt. The average American owes $9,000 on his credit cards alone and he's lucky if he is just able to stay ahead of the bills. Only 1 percent of Americans are able to put some money away for savings. On top of all that, every American (man, woman, and child) owes $80,000 to Uncle Sam to pay off our insidious national debt. Over the past five years, the average total household debt (mortgages included) has soared from 60 percent to 75 percent of annual disposable income. These are just a few of the debt numbers that can make anyone become discouraged. Rather than dwell on them, let's get an overview of your situation.

#1. What is the primary cause of personal debt?

Excessive spending is the primary cause. It has become as addictive as alcohol or drugs in this country. Like alcohol or drugs, debts can interfere with every aspect of your life including damaging relationships with those who mean the most to you. Americans owe more money now than ever before. As you read through this chapter and assess your current debt situation, take an honest look at your spending habits. Do you have a spending plan that's written down and that you follow? How much are you spending every month by expense categories? Before you can solve any of your debt problems, you need to understand how you got into trouble in the first place. If you don't take the time to determine how you got into debt, then in all probability, you will repeat the same mistake again and again.

Think back to the point in time when you were able to live on your salary without having to borrow extra money. What happened that sparked your debt problem? Maybe you lost your job? Was it when you bought that fantastic car that you couldn't afford? When the issuer doubled the credit limit on your credit card, did you go on a spending spree? Maybe your debt problem was caused by a combination of things.

#2. **Exactly what is personal debt and how does it affect my credit?**

Debt is the amount of money you owe someone, to be paid off usually with interest within a specific time period. It's money that you have already spent, to be paid back with dollars that you will earn in the future. Credit is the opposite of debt. It represents the potential to borrow money to buy something. When you use credit, you create debt and when you pay off debt, you create credit. Maintaining a healthy balance between the use of debt and credit is a critical component of a sound money management plan.

Credit is generally thought of as a good thing and most debt is considered a bad thing. Some people get confused about this relationship. They'll acquire all the credit cards they can so that they can display them to their friends and brag about how much credit they have. At the same time, they will run up excessive debt to impress lenders about their ability to repay loans. Needless to say, that is not the way to impress lenders.

#3. **How do I determine if I have a serious debt problem?**

People with serious debt problems often panic and move too fast to solve a problem that has been with them for years. They'll quickly pay off the wrong kinds of debt without assessing their entire financial situation. In most cases, short-term fixes won't make their debt problems disappear. To determine if you have a problem, check the following warning signs. If three or more signs apply, you may have a serious debt problem.

1. Always juggling payments or stalling one creditor to pay another and consistently receiving past due notices on your bills.
2. Failing to save a consistent amount of money each month. You're unable to save at least 5 percent of your paycheck each payday.
3. Charging more each month than you make in debt payments and having more than five credit cards.
4. Taking longer and longer to pay off your debts and using credit card cash advances to make payments on other debt accounts.
5. Always running out of money before payday and bouncing checks on a recurring basis.
6. Not knowing how much money you owe and searching through your junk mail to find applications for new credit cards.
7. Charging purchases like groceries that you used to pay for in cash.
8. Paying the bare minimum allowed on your debts (e.g., credit cards) every month.

#4. **What do people who get into debt have in common?**

People who get into excessive debt are all addicted to overspending. The inappropriate use of loans and credit cards is one of the primary reasons why people encounter major debt problems. When their wallet is nearly empty and their checkbook balance is low, they should know they're nearing their spending limit. But if they can easily turn to their credit cards, they can go into an overspending mode without realizing it until the bills start coming in.

Good credit management requires planning and constant monitoring. Take a look at your current credit situation. Do you know how much you pay out each month on credit cards and loan obligations? Are your total debts in line with your disposable income, which is the dollars you have left after taxes have been deducted from your paycheck? (Less than 10 percent is recommended.) Do you have money in a savings account that you can use to cover financial emergencies such as a job loss or sudden medical bills?

If your credit picture isn't clear in your mind, it's time to organize your thoughts and take a closer look at where you're going financially. Overspending and living beyond one's means combined with a lack of awareness, self-control, and commitment will create excessive debt at an alarming pace. You can access a debt calculator at *http://cgi.money.cnn.com/tools/debtplanner/debtplanner.jsp* that will help you project when you will be debt free.

#5. **Why do a lot of people fail to ever get out of debt?**

People who are always in debt refuse to set up and actively maintain a monthly budget. The term "budgeting" makes their blood run cold. You'll often hear them say, "There is no way I will ever start maintaining a budget because I don't want to know how bad off I am financially." Unless you were raised by financially conscious parents, the disciplinary act of budgeting and being accountable for what you spend is a scary process for most people to consider. For many, it uncovers the reality that they don't have enough money to make ends meet. Overspending demands that they need to immediately start spending less, that they stop buying all the things that they believe they can't live without. Unfortunately, they are not willing to do that and would prefer to remain in debt for the rest of their lives. You can view a sample budget on the Internet at *www .personalbudgeting.com*.

#6. Why am I paying more for a loan just because I owe more than what I should?

If your potential creditors believe that you have accumulated an excessive amount of debt, they will either refuse to extend a loan to you or they will charge you high interest rates. This determination is made from your credit score, which is disclosed to them by credit agencies. Your creditworthiness is based on your payment history, income, potential debt, and the number of years you have been employed. The best score is 850, and 300 is the lowest score you can have. For a small fee, you can find out what your score is at *www.myfico.com*.

#7. Is bankruptcy a good alternative way to get out of debt?

If your financial situation seems hopeless, you may want to consider bankruptcy as a way out. Before you file for bankruptcy, discuss the consequences with your spouse, close family members, and friends. Regardless of what you may have heard, bankruptcy is not a simple solution. Your credit rating will be severely tarnished for seven to ten years and you will be required to pay high interest rates on any loans that you're able to get after declaring bankruptcy.

When filing for bankruptcy, you file for a petition under the federal bankruptcy law. Although you can file by yourself, you are much better off retaining the services of a bankruptcy attorney. You and your attorney draw up a petition listing your assets and liabilities. You submit the petition to a U.S. District Court judge, and if the judge accepts your petition, some of your assets could be sold by the court to pay off your creditors. The court then wipes out most or all of your debts except:

- Alimony and child support
- Most state and federal taxes

- Most federal student loans
- Any debt not listed on your bankruptcy petition

If you are interested in learning more about bankruptcy, visit the website *www.bankruptcyinfo.com* and see Chapter 8.

#8. Is there such a thing as good debt?

There are two basic types of debt: unsecured debt and secured debt. Unsecured debts are those that are not backed by collateral. Because there are no assets behind unsecured loans, lenders realize a bigger risk from borrowers and therefore charge a higher interest rate for the loan. Credit card debts and personal loans are examples of unsecured loans. Secured debts are backed with collateral, which reduces a lender's risk. They can therefore charge a lower interest rate for the loan. For this reason, secured debts are considered good or preferred debt over unsecured debts. Home mortgages and most car loans are examples of secured loans.

#9. What can I do now to begin getting out of debt?

Getting out of debt when you're "up to your neck" in bills may make the goal seem impossible to reach. You may have taken out several easy payment loans when your income was in line with your expenses. But now, with the cost of everything on the rise, those once-easy payments are harder to make. To get out of debt, stop charging your purchases and do not open new credit accounts. If you are not sure you have the willpower to stop charging, remove all of the credit cards in your wallet and cut each one of them into small pieces.

#10. What is a spending plan and do I need one?

A spending plan shows you how you will spend your money on a daily, weekly, and monthly basis. It is itemized down to what you plan to spend on any given day. Do you need one? The answer to the question is an emphatic YES. If you don't have a plan that's in writing (one in your head doesn't qualify as a plan), you will sub-stantially reduce your chances of ever getting out of debt.

One of the first things you need to do to set up a spending plan is to determine what your credit limit should be. The total limit available to you may be more than you can handle. It's up to you to establish the credit limit that is acceptable to you and record that number in your plan. One way to determine what your personal credit limit should be is to figure out how much you can afford to pay each month for credit purchases. Review your monthly debt payments as well as your total outstanding debt. Once you establish your personal credit limit, plan your credit spending so that your total payments do not exceed this amount. If you are interested in learning more about "getting out of debt" plans, visit Quicken's website at *www.quicken.com/planning/debt*.

#11. If I decide to set up and maintain a spending plan, what will it help me accomplish?

A spending plan is an active strategy you use on a daily basis to help control your spending habits so that you can meet your financial goals. It starts with a commitment you make to yourself, like: "I want to save and invest some of my income to live better and become financially independent." When you activate your plan, it will help you discriminate between what you need and what you want. Here are three things a spending plan will help you accomplish:

- It helps you plan and prepare for the big expenses like a new car and helps you eliminate the unnecessary things you might otherwise buy without planning.
- It will put more money into your savings account for invest-ments every month. It sets the groundwork for developing a financial plan, your road map to financial independence.
- It gets you used to living on what you make and gets you, your spouse, and your kids pulling in the same financial direction.

Chapter 2

DETERMINING WHERE YOU WANT TO GO

People often take a hasty approach in solving their debt problem. As a result, they end up paying off the wrong debts, in the wrong order, and at the expense of more important financial matters. A better approach is to first assess your overall financial situation before you start challenging your debt. You can't make smart debt management decisions in a vacuum. Your other financial goals like retirement can have a profound impact on which debts you pay off and how quickly. Make sure you have enough saved up to cover financial emergencies like car repairs. This chapter will help you determine where you want to go and what the best way is to get there.

#12. How do I start to understand my debts?

To get started, you need to know exactly what you owe by account. For each debt, write down the current balance owed and whether the loan is an installment or revolving loan. Revolving debt includes credit cards where you have a credit limit that you can draw on. Paying off revolving loans generally increases your financial flexibility because you can always draw on that freed-up credit line if you need it. What is the interest rate you're paying and is the rate fixed or variable? Credit cards are typically variable since the rates can change at any time. Installment loans usually have a fixed rate unless you took out an adjustable-rate loan (e.g., a home mortgage). Installment loans include mortgages and car loans where you have a set schedule of payments to make and a specific payoff date. An installment loan is for a specific purpose and is gradually repaid in full—there is no freed-up credit line to draw from. Is the interest on a given loan tax-deductible? If you pay a loan off, are there any prepayment penalties? What is the minimum amount you are allowed to pay for each loan? Your worksheet might look something like the following:

Debt Repayment Worksheet

Debt	Balance Owed	Type	Interest Rate	Minimum Payment	Typical Payment
Mortgage	$150,000	Fixed	6.5%	$2,500/month	$2,500/month
Home equity line of credit	$25,000	Fixed	5%	$500/month	$500/month
Student loan	N/A				
Credit card 1	$3,400	Variable	13.9%	$40.00	$150.00
Credit card 2	$2,200	Variable	8.9%	$25.00	$100.00
Auto loan 1	$17,000	Fixed	6.99%	$407.00	$407.00
Auto loan 2	$14,000	Fixed	6.99%	$335.00	$335.00

#13. How do I determine where I am and where I want to go financially?

Go through your bank statement and write down what you spent your money on over the past three months (e.g., food, entertainment, credit card interest, living expenses, etc.). How much money did you make, and did you have enough to cover all of your expenses? Did you spend more than you made? If you spent less than you made, what did you do with the extra money? That exercise should help you determine where you are today.

Now, where do you want to go? Set meaningful, specific financial goals, with a designated completion date assigned to them. For example, if your goal is to reduce your debt by $10 a day so that you can pay off a credit card, what steps will you take to make it happen and when will you start? If you are living above your means, figure out a way to live within your means. You must figure out how to live on what you make if you want to gain control of your finances.

#14. **What are some of the steps I can take to reduce my expenses?**

For most people, cutting expenses is a lot easier than raising their income to get out of debt. Name any expense that you have and there is probably a way to reduce it. The following lists will help you get started on expense areas to consider.

Housing and utilities
Opt for higher deductibles on your homeowners or renters insurance.
Turn your thermostat down in the winter and up in the summer.
Drop premium channels from your television and telephone service.

Transportation
Increase the deductibles on your auto insurance policy.
Start carpooling to work and use public transportation.

Food
Pack a lunch to work and eliminate eating out at fast-food restaurants.
Use weekly grocery store circulars to see what's on sale and plan your meals accordingly.

Clothing
Check out consignment and thrift stores for gently used items.
Know what looks good on you, and stick to classic styles rather than chasing trends.

#15. **What are some of the areas that I need to consider to make some extra money?**

At a minimum, you should be able to identify money-saving plays that you can put into your game plan. First determine how you can make some extra money. Getting rid of an unneeded vehicle could allow you to raise some significant cash to retire some of your debts and reduce monthly expenses. Perhaps a yard sale is what you need to get rid of the clutter around the house and make some money at the same time. Have you thought about taking a part-time job? Check out every overtime option where you work. Read the "part-time" work ads in the classified sections of the local newspapers to find an opportunity to make some extra money.

#16. **What is a financial planner, and do I need one?**

A financial planner makes a living assisting people in developing and implementing customized financial plans. A good financial planner works with you on an ongoing basis to help build your portfolio. Certified financial planners must take a five-part course, pass a ten-hour exam, and complete fifteen hours of additional training a year to become certified. Many financial planners have security licenses, which allow them to sell you the financial products they recommend. Most of us don't need the services of a professional financial planner on an ongoing basis. A periodic consultation with your accountant may be sufficient to manage your debt since basic financial planning isn't hard to do. Under certain circumstances, you may need to work with a financial planner on a recurring basis if:

1. You earn a good wage but cannot manage to save anything on a regular basis, or, to make matters worse, you don't even know where all your money is going.
2. You're facing a tough financial question that you feel can't be answered without some expert advice. For example, your company is "downsizing" and has offered you an early retirement buyout. However, you still have fifteen years left in your career. Should you take it? You may need advice from a financial planner.

3. You've got a savings and retirement plan in place that is just sitting there without any help from you and it's making some money. Should you leave it alone or start playing an active role in managing your investments with the help of a financial planner?

#17. Will inflation help me get out of debt?

Americans unfortunately have been sucked into the inflation scenario: "Finance now and pay off later with cheaper dollars." That might work if your income increased at the same rate as or a greater rate than inflation. Unfortunately, for most of us, it never has and probably never will. Stagnant economic conditions resulting from significant price spikes in the necessities of life like gasoline and food always add to the debt burden of everybody because inflation erodes the buying power of everybody's paycheck. Don't let yourself get sucked into the "buy it now before the price goes up" hype or you'll just dig yourself into a deeper debt hole.

#18. How might my financial outlook change as I get older?

As you progress through life—which is a diplomatic way of saying "as you get older"—your financial needs will change. When you're young, the last thing you probably want to think about is retiring. You're more concerned about buying a house, raising a family, and acquiring all the material things that you deserve. As you get older, you will face a crossroad in your life. You can either continue to acquire more material things or you can start making an effort to plan for your future by saving money for your retirement. If you wait until you get older to start saving, time is not on your side.

#19. Do banks have money management counselors who are worth talking to?

Yes, but you will have a tough time getting access to one. Most big banks are focused on delivering profits to their investors at the expense of the customer service that they're willing to provide for their "regular" customers. Unless you can bring an exceptional amount of business into the bank or make a substantial deposit, you won't have access to their money management staff. Small local and regional banks might offer you more personal finance services and advice. At a minimum, you will need a checking account with some form of overdraft protection, a savings account, direct deposit options, a debit card option as opposed to a credit card, and free access to conveniently located ATMs.

#20. **Are there questionable get-out-of-debt deals that I should avoid?**

Beware of those "experts" who con people into quick get-out-of-debt schemes. Get-rich-quick e-mails, investments that can't lose, gambling, and even chain letters may tempt you off the slow and steady path to getting out of debt. Just remember that every dollar you waste on a fly-by-night solution is a dollar that won't get you closer to your goal. Call the nonprofit Consumer Credit Counseling Service (800-388-CCCS) for help. Most of their 1,300 national offices offer free counseling and will help you trim your expenses, plan a budget, and even help you negotiate better terms from your creditors.

#21. **Is my standard of living disrupting my ability to get out of debt?**

The two prevalent reasons most people fail to get out of debt are (1) they lack the personal commitment to make it happen and (2) they can't control their excessive spending habit to fit within a standard of living that they can afford. They continue to write checks and charge credit cards without any regard for how they're going to pay for it. They are infatuated with doing whatever it takes to maintain their perceived high standard of living in the short run with little or no thought for the long-term consequences of their actions. They'd rather not think about the long term. Once they get used to their short-term standard of living, they are caught up in a vicious circle.

Their short-term debt gets bigger and bigger, and their long-term financial needs get farther and farther away.

#22. **What can I do to motivate myself to get out of debt?**

Getting out of debt can be a rewarding personal challenge, if you reflect on the alternative. Think about the issues and consequences for a moment. You have gotten used to a certain lifestyle, a standard of living. The very thought of confronting your debt to improve upon your financial situation may not sit well with you. Changing spending habits and saving money are probably something that you can quickly talk yourself out of doing. Why not leave well enough alone? Now ask yourself, are you happy living beyond your means? Are you comfortable with being a debtor for the rest of your life? Do your dismal financial affairs affect your personal life? If you want to achieve more with your life, then reach deep inside yourself and awaken one of the most powerful drives we humans have: motivation. The motivational process starts when you make an ironclad commitment to yourself to get out of debt.

Chapter **3**

LIVING ON A BUDGET

Everyone should have a budget, even millionaires. It is critical to know where your money is coming from and where it is going. By monitoring your spending habits, you will begin to identify areas where cost savings can occur. You will then be able to create a budget that is conducive to helping you get out of debt and keep your spending on the right track. Many consider budgeting to be a tedious task, but it really doesn't have to be. Once you set it up, it can be easy and even fun to maintain.

#23. What is the difference between a budget and a spending plan?

A spending plan is an active strategy that you use to get out of debt. It needs to be written down and have simple milestones to show you how you're doing. Spending plans are designed to help you gain control over your daily expenses. Excess spending is usually a result of (1) uncontrolled or impulse spending and (2) a failure to realize how much things cost. Impulse spenders buy first and consider the consequences later. Creating and maintaining a spending plan is the first step you need to take, before you develop a budget. If you are not able to control your daily expenses, then preparing a budget would be a waste of your time.

The budget is an expanded spending plan in which you methodically project what your anticipated income and expenses will be over a specified period of time. This is typically done on a monthly basis. Record everything you buy in a budget book so you know where you are at any time during the month. This will help keep you from getting that surprised look on your face at the end of the month when you get your bills and say, "Wow, I didn't realize I spent that much." Put a limit on what you are willing to charge each month and stick to it. Pay off the balance that you run up at the end of every month.

#24. What are the primary components of a monthly budget?

Here are the major components of a budget:

> **Disposable income** is your gross income less withholdings for taxes, health insurance, FICA, etc.

> **Major obligations** are regular expenses that are usually contractual like rent and mortgage payments, car loans, property taxes, and day care and school expenses. Obligation expenses are anything that must be paid before you can consider other expenses.

> **Necessities** are important expenses such as groceries, utilities, and home maintenance that can be adjusted through tight money management techniques.

> **Credit card payments** are the total monthly payments you need to make on all of your cards.

> **Discretionary expenses** can be significantly modified or eliminated altogether and include entertainment, take-out food, pocket money, family allowances, etc.

> **Savings** is the final component of the budget and shows what you will do with any money that's left over after all expenses have been paid.

#25. **What are the five steps that I need to take in preparing a budget?**

Step 1: Understand where your income comes from and where it goes. What about the income that you may receive periodically from sources such as tax refunds, overtime, or a garage sale? How do you plan to use it in your budget? The same goes for unplanned expenses like repairs on your car. Are those types of expenses addressed in your budget?

Step 2: What are your short- and long-term budget goals? For example, if you are planning to buy a new television with cash, do you have an entry in your budget that shows how much you plan to save each payday to make that happen?

Step 3: Do you have a savings mechanism set up in your budget? For example, if you plan to create an emergency savings account to cover such things as unexpected car repairs, have you opened a savings account for that purpose?

Step 4: Most of us need some amount of pocket money to fund everyday expenses. Address how much each member of your family needs and gets in separate lines within your budget.

Step 5: Review your budget on a regular basis (at least once a week is recommended). Compare actual sources of incoming income against expenses. Were your income and expenses in line with what you forecast in your budget? If you were over or under budget, what happened and what is your plan of action?

#26. **Does my budget need to be in writing?**

Yes. You may think you can remember it all, but having it written down is a much more effective method. Every time you review it by yourself or with family members, you will want to record actual income and expense figures next to your budgetary figures. In some cases, you may be able to take immediate action to mitigate a budget problem. Your action plan needs to be spelled out in your budget as a reminder not to repeat the same mistakes in the future.

#27. Why do people fail to stay within their budget?

Most budgets fail because they never really get started. Here is what happens in a typical "yeah, let's go on a budget" scenario. In their excitement to figure out a way to get out of debt, people often buy a "how to set up a budget" book and hastily create a budget. A short time later, they may actually sit down and review what they actually spent versus what they said they would spend in their budget. When budget dollars don't match actual dollars, they quickly conclude that the budget idea was just a waste of time, and they go back to doing what they have always done— running up more debt.

#28. Why do people buy a lot of stuff that they really don't need?

Competing with the Joneses is one reason. There is always a "latest and greatest" product that some people must have regardless of the cost. For example, look at how flat-screen televisions have expanded in size and cost the past couple of years. Or the latest, hottest, fastest computer and cell phone technology. One of the keys in controlling debt is to hold off on any frivolous spending. Apply any extra money you may have to paying off your debt before you accumulate more debt. According to *SmartMoney* magazine, in 2009 the debt per American household (excluding mortgages) is $21,900. Avoid this trap by adhering to your budget.

#29. How can I get my spouse and family to commit to a monthly budget?

No budget is going to work if you don't have a commitment from everybody in your family to support it. As a general rule, people are much more willing to endorse a solution to a problem if they are involved in coming up with the solution. Actively solicit their thoughts and incorporate any of their helpful ideas in your final budget. Make sure that everyone who's involved in the process understands that no budget is final. It has to be a dynamic tool that can and will change over time. Let your family know that you want them to be actively involved in those changes. Rewards for their help and commitment like going out to the family's favorite restaurant can help.

#30. What's the best way to maintain a budget?

Find a good resource or tool that is available for you to implement right away. For example, SimplePlanning.com at *www.simple planning.net* has a program that is downloadable for a small fee. If you are using Microsoft Office, consider using the financial templates that are included in the program. Any financial planning tool that will help organize your spending and make the process less demanding on your personal time is worthwhile.

#31. What should I do if I spend more than what's in my budget?

On the minor stuff, take notes and move on to the bigger issues. For example, many utility bills are impossible to estimate to the penny. The fact that your electric bill was $20 over what you had budgeted is not a major budget issue. Simply make a note of it and determine whether you want to increase the budget amount next month or implement a plan to use less electricity. On the other hand, if the minimum payment on one of your credit cards increases by $20 from $100 to $120, take notice. That same $20 increase probably occurred because major debt of several hundred dollars was added to the total balance due on the card. Where did it come from, and was it a result of unplanned expenses? How did it happen? These are just a few of the tough budget questions you need to address before you can implement a preventive plan.

#32. **My friend tells me that if you borrow what you need, you don't need a budget. What exactly does that mean?**

That means your friend probably has a lot of debt. Do you know someone who likes to brag about borrowing whatever she needs? She will tell you that that is why she doesn't need a budget. And that is why she is buried in debt. The question that she should be asking is how much she can afford to borrow. If she wanted to get out of debt, then her answer should probably be zero. Be extremely wary of increasing any one of your budget items that pushes you further into debt.

Chapter 4

AVOIDING DEBT TRAPS

When your wallet is nearly empty and your checkbook balance is low, you know you're nearing your spending limit. But if you can easily turn to credit, you are more likely to overspend without realizing it—until the bills start coming in. Most financial counselors recommend that you should stop charging when your credit payments (not including a mortgage) approach 15 percent of your take-home pay. If you're beyond that, you have fallen into the debt trap.

#33. What are the most common debt traps?

Inappropriate use of credit and loans can become one of your biggest financial downfalls.

To determine whether you owe too much, check the following warning signs to see if any apply to you:

- You're always juggling payments or stalling one creditor to pay another.
- You're consistently receiving past due notices on your bills.
- You're failing to save a set amount of money each month.
- You're charging more each month than you make in monthly payments.
- You're taking longer and longer to pay off your debts.

#34. I'm spending every dime I make. What can I do to get my expenses in line with what I make?

This is where your budget will come in handy. Understanding your expenses and where they are coming from is your first step in getting them under control. The budget will help you to outline your expenses and identify any areas that can be eliminated. For example, do you really need to have Starbucks coffee every day? At $3 a day, that's $1,095 a year! Budgeting will also flag some necessary expenses, and you can begin to think about how you can decrease them.

#35. Are there immediate steps that I can take now to stop borrowing?

You can assess every loan to be sure it addresses a valid need in your life. Why do we borrow money? Most of the time, it is because we want something. On occasion, we borrow money because we need something. In the personal finance world, there is a huge difference between the words "want something" and "need something." You need to understand that difference if you want to gain control over your borrowing habits. For example, you may need a car or some other form of transportation to get to work. That's a necessity.

However, what you want overrides your need. You *want* a new car, complete with a powerful engine that is capable of catapulting you from zero to 60 miles per hour in less than five seconds. People borrow money to buy what they want, rather than what they need, without regard to the consequences. Stop borrowing for stuff you just want. If you really want it badly enough, save the cash to buy it! A typical new car loan now takes five to six years to pay back. Do you have a savings account set up to cover you for emergencies during those years?

#36. What are the symptoms of a bad loan?

High interest that you are paying for a loan is the chief symptom that it's bad. Let say you borrow $1,000 to be paid off over forty-eight months at 18 percent interest. It will cost you $410 in interest over the term of the loan. That's 41 percent or nearly half of the amount that you borrowed just for interest. The terms of a loan can be another symptom. Many bad loans require you to pay late payment fees that are exorbitant (typically 35 percent or higher in interest rates).

#37. How can I figure out what a loan really costs?

Many factors go into figuring out the full cost of a loan. Be sure to add:

- The interest paid
- Late payment fees, which can easily exceed $30 per occurrence
- Interest rate increases, which can be triggered by any number of events that are spelled out in the "extra fine print" in the contract that you signed
- Prepayment penalties, which you may be required to pay should you desire to get out from under a loan

#38. Should I consider a rent-to-own deal?

Whether you are buying a television, furniture, or a computer, rent-to-own stores will charge you a substantial premium for the privilege of paying over time. For example, let's assume that you have agreed to pay a minor sum of $20 a week over the next fifty-two weeks or a total of $1,040 for your new television. If you had paid cash, that same TV would have cost you $700. By accepting the deal, you ended up paying the retailer 48 percent interest ($1,040/$700) for their rent-to-own deal. What a deal for them!

#39. Are loans secured by my car's title a debt trap?

Yes. Pink slip loans, as they are called, are secured by the equity (value) you have in your car. You're required to give the lender your title and often a spare set of keys to consummate the loan. Title loans typically carry exorbitant interest rates. If you are late on your loan payment by even one day, the lender has the legal right to confiscate your car. If you borrowed less than what your car was worth, the lender still gets to keep all the proceeds after they sell your car. The lender may require you to carry excessive insurance on your car (e.g., collision, theft, uninsured motorist coverage) that you normally would not have. Additional insurance costs need to be added to what you're being charged for interest and finance charges so that you can determine what you're really paying for the loan. In most cases, it won't be worth it.

#40. **What are refund anticipation loans?**

A refund anticipation loan is a loan a lender makes under the expectation that you will be able to pay it back with a refund that you are expecting to receive. Some "storefront" tax preparers will offer a client a loan for an amount equal to their anticipated refund less a few fees right after they have completed a tax return. The fees they charge you can be significant (i.e., 25 percent or more of the refund). For example, let's suppose that you have just had your tax return prepared and you are eligible to receive a $1,000 refund for overpaying your taxes. Your tax preparer offers you the following deal: Pay me a $20 fee now and I will give you a $1,000 check for your refund. Had you elected to file your return electronically, you could have gotten your refund in a couple of weeks. Let's assume that you accepted the deal. What did it end up costing you? Just 2 percent ($20/$1,000 = 2 percent) for the two-week loan or the equivalent of 1 percent a week—but wait a minute. You really paid the equivalent of 52 percent on an annualized basis (1% × 52 weeks/year = 52%). The two-week wait for your tax refund would have been well worth it.

#41. **What can I do to avoid foreclosure?**

If you are facing the possibility of a foreclosure on your home, it is important that you understand that nobody wins in a foreclosure. The borrower gets a bad credit record and the lender wastes a lot of time and money going through the foreclosure process. That gives you a fighting chance of avoiding foreclosure. Call your lender as soon as you get a foreclosure notice. Explain why you're having difficulty making payments and what you will do to catch up to avoid foreclosure to resolve the problem. Be prepared to provide financial details of your monthly income and expenses. Options that you may want to consider are:

- Refinance even at a higher interest rate if it will lower your monthly payments.
- Ask the lender for permission to make partial payments. Some lenders will allow you to do this for a short time.
- Ask for a modification to your existing loan. Perhaps you can pay back what you owe at the same interest rate over a longer period of time to reduce your monthly payments.

#42. Should I avoid the get-out-of-debt schemes that come my way?

Yes. The fees for get-out-of-debt loans are typically outrageous, and the loans usually just stretch out your payments, costing you much more than if you had paid off the original debt. The get-out-of-debt companies are riddled with fraud and phony come-ons that are designed to part you from whatever money you have left.

Chapter **5**

CHECKING YOUR CREDIT SCORE

Unfortunately, debt has become the high-octane fuel that powers our economy and funds the lifestyle of many individuals. The advent of consumer credit and the resulting debt has created a system for creating and maintaining a credit score on every debtor in the country. The more you know about your own score and how it's maintained, the better off you will be to make sure it is used in your best interest.

#43. Exactly what is a credit score, and how is it used?

Most loans are based on your credit score, which is a three-digit number that lenders use to help determine your creditworthiness. Credit score is a snapshot of your credit history at any moment in time that indicates to lenders the likelihood you will default on your loan payments. The most common score is known as the Fair Isaac Corporation, or FICO, score that ranges from a low score of 560 points to a high of 800 points. The higher your score, the better will be the interest rates and terms you'll get on a loan.

Your credit score is used by the lender to determine how much he is willing to lend you and what interest rate he will charge.

Obviously, if your credit score is below his minimum score, he won't lend you anything. Your credit score can also affect the rates you'll have to pay for homeowners and auto insurance. It can also affect whether or not you'll get hired for a particular job (for example, a money-handling position). The bottom line is that your credit score is a powerful piece of information that can work for or against you, so manage it well.

#44. Who do I contact to find out what my credit score is?

The three major credit bureaus to contact for your report are:

- Equifax Information Service Center, P.O. Box 740241, Atlanta, GA 30374 (800-686-1111 or *www.equifax.com*)
- Experian Consumer Assistance (formerly TRW), P.O. Box 2104, Allen, TX 75013 (800-397-3742 or *www .experian.com*)
- Trans Union Corp., Consumer Disclosure Center, P.O. Box 390, Springfield, PA 19064 (800-916-8800 or *www .transunion.com*)

#45. What can I do to improve my credit score?

First, look for errors and outdated information that may be causing your score to be lower than it should be. If you find any errors, notify the appropriate bureau in writing of any necessary corrections (see Question 47 for more information).

Make sure you have a checking and a savings account. Lenders view these accounts as a minimum sign of stability. Make sure these accounts are recorded on your credit report. Have at least one credit card that you are using in good standing (no late payments, not maxed out, etc.). If you have a credit score above 620, you will begin to get favorable rates on the money you borrow. You need a score above 720 to qualify for the best rates—though in times of severe credit crunch, even that may not be enough.

#46. How does bankruptcy affect one's credit score?

Bankruptcy should only be used as a last-ditch effort because it will ruin your credit (FICO) score for years. A bankruptcy stays on your credit report for seven to ten years—that's a long time to go with severely limited credit. Any loans that you might be able to get during this time will likely be charged the highest interest rate that is allowed in your state.

#47. If I disagree with anything that's on my credit report, what action can I take?

Credit bureaus get your credit status from creditors, who report your payment history to the bureaus. If creditors make a mistake, it goes on your record. Minor errors are usually not very important, but a major mistake like showing a tax lien against you that belongs to someone else can take months to resolve, and your credit can be cut off while the problem is getting resolved. A recent study by the U.S. Department of Commerce showed that 75 percent of the consumer credit files that they randomly audited contained at least one major error. If you review your credit report for errors, make sure you check the following:

- All of your identification information including your social security number, date of birth, current and past addresses, and current and former employers and their addresses.
- All account numbers and correct status (active or closed) and your payment record history, with an emphasis on checking late payment marks.

In the event that you discover an error, write the credit bureau to request that the error be corrected. Attach whatever documentation you may have to back up your claim. Under federal law, they are required to respond to your request within thirty days.

#48. **What is a good credit score and what can it do for me?**

What is a good credit score? The qualified answer to that question depends in part on where your score has been, where you want it to go, and how you plan on using it. If your score is less than 625, you will have a difficult time getting a legitimate lender to loan you money. The vast majority of people have scores that exceed 625. A score of 700 or higher (800 is the highest) is a good credit score. It will allow you to qualify for the best interest rate on both secured and unsecured loans. Higher credit scores are needed to qualify for home mortgages. Lenders are reluctant to give a thirty-year fixed-rate mortgage to someone with a low score. Your high score shows that you have "staying power" for a long-term loan. Auto loans are a bit more lenient because they are short-term (six years or less) loans. The more credit cards you have listed on your credit report the lower your score, even if the cards are paid off. That's because they suggest that you can quickly max out your credit limit if you use them. You are better off having just one major credit card.

Chapter **6**

CONSOLIDATING DEBTS

Consolidating your debts means taking two or more debts and rolling them up into a single lump sum debt that's hopefully at a lower interest rate with favorable terms. Unfortunately, some people use it as a convenient way of wiping out the balances of a bunch of credit cards so that they can begin using them again. That can be very dangerous to their overall debt situation. They're not just right back where they started from; they are worse off because they now have to pay back both loans. Don't let that happen to you if you decide to consolidate your debts.

#49. How should the interest rates that I'm paying on my debts affect my decision to consolidate?

Let's say you are carrying $10,000 in credit card debts at 18 percent. If you decide to pay $150 each month to pay them off, it will take you twenty-four years. If you were able to get a consolidation loan for, say, 6 percent and continued to pay $150 a month, you would pay your cards off in eight years. That is one of the main reasons why a well-thought-out and executed debt consolidation plan at the right interest rate may help you get out of debt.

#50. **How do I get started implementing a consolidation plan?**

If you decide to consolidate your debt, you need to assure yourself that you will not use consolidation as a way to run up more debt. Make sure you are prepared to, at a minimum, do the following:

1. Get rid of all but one or two low-rate credit cards. Take those credit cards out of your wallet and replace them with a debit card. Store them in an out-of-the-way place and only use them for legitimate financial emergencies.
2. Start paying cash for everything. If you can't pay cash, you should have a good reason, such as your car breaks down. Use a debit card instead of a credit card whenever you can.
3. Actively solicit the help and advice of your family and friends with regard to what you are trying to accomplish with your consolidation plan. For example, after you have shown them your plan, solicit their advice and be accountable to them to help you stay on track.

#51. **I have some equity in my home. What are home equity loans all about?**

Home equity loans, home equity lines of credit, and cash-out refinancing are the three primary ways to consolidate your debt. Here is a summary of what they are:

1. Home equity loans are fixed-rate loans. They are typically available in terms ranging from five to fifteen years. When you take out a home equity loan, you borrow the money all at once and start repaying it immediately.
2. Home equity lines of credit loans are variable-rate loans with interest rates that are tied to the prime rate with terms ranging from five to ten years. You receive a checkbook and can withdraw funds up to your credit limit and start repaying it immediately.

3. Cash-out refinancing is when you refinance your home because it has more equity in it than when you originally bought it. You are paid a lump-sum amount when the loan goes through that is the home's equity (i.e., appreciation) less any loan fees.

#52. When does it pay to refinance your mortgage?

The mortgage loan experts will tell you to consider refinancing your mortgage when interest rates drop two percentage points below your current rate. Waiting for that kind of drop to help you lower your monthly mortgage payments could take some time. Before you pursue a refinance option, you will need to get answers to the following questions:

- Given the current rates, how much will you save each month after you refinance?
- How much will it cost to refinance, and will you be in your home long enough to make it worthwhile?
- Is the term of the proposed refinance plan the same as or less than your current mortgage term?

Armed with the answers to these questions, you can quickly determine if it will be worth your while to refinance. Let's assume that it will cost you $2,000 to refinance your home, but your monthly payments will drop $100, a savings of $1,200 a year. It'll take you twenty months to break even, before the real savings begin ($2,000/$1,200 × 12 months = 20 months). If you move before the twenty months are up, you lose money by refinancing. Stay longer and you will have the advantage financially. Also keep in mind that the $1,200 a year you save is a tax deduction you can no longer take. If you're in the 25 percent tax bracket, that amounts to $300 (25% × $1,200) less that you'll get back at the end of each tax year. Therefore, your real savings may not be $1,200 a year but rather $900 ($1,200 − $300). It now takes you almost twenty-seven months ($1,200/$900 × 12 months = 27 months) to break even.

#53. **How do I figure out which debts to pay off first?**

The general answer is that you pay off your most expensive loans first, the ones that are charging you the highest interest rates. However, it's not a hard-and-fast rule. For example, if a lower-rate card has the highest balance and the largest monthly finance charge, you'll want to pay that down first. If you are considering paying off one of two loans where Loan A is charging you 8 percent and Loan B is charging you 10 percent, it makes sense to pay off Loan B. But what if the interest that you're paying on Loan B is tax deductible (i.e., for a second mortgage) and you are in the 30 percent tax bracket—is that still prudent? The after-tax interest that you are really paying for Loan B is 7 percent rather than 10 percent. In this case, it may be to your advantage to pay off Loan A. A prepayment penalty on a loan could also determine if it makes economic sense to pay it off versus another higher-interest loan with no prepayment penalty.

#54. **Are there any consolidation scam schemes that I should avoid?**

At any moment in time, someone is creating a scam for people who are desperately trying to get out of debt. Deal only with known debt consolidation companies in your area. Ask for references from their clients before you make any serious commitments. If you are being asked to pay a fee to start a debt consolidation program, raise your guard. Ask what the fee covers and what happens after you pay the fee. If you don't get answers that you are completely satisfied with, take a walk.

#55. **Should I consider switching from one credit card to another credit card?**

Credit card companies are notorious with their direct mail and e-mail campaigns that entice you to consolidate all of your credit cards under their one universal credit card. Are they a good deal? Yes, if you can in fact transfer your high interest rate cards to a lower interest rate card. However, make sure you understand what the new card is proposing to do for you. Read all of the fine print in the material that they sent to you and get the answers to the following questions:

- What lower interest rate will they charge you and for how long will it remain in effect?
- What are the annual fees and any other special fees for which you will be responsible?
- What are your credit limits and restrictions on the new card?
- When the rate the new card is offering you expires (they usually do), what interest rate will you be charged?

Chapter 7

SPENDING LESS

To figure out a way to start spending less, you must first know what you're spending now. Although this may sound like a no-brainer, many people don't fully comprehend that they spend more money than they make. A September 2008 survey conducted by *Money* magazine revealed over half of the people surveyed don't pay off their credit card bills each month, 70 percent don't save on a regular basis, and 60 percent don't want to know how bad off they are financially.

#56. **What can I do to control my urge to always spend money?**

For many, shopping has become a social event, a chance to get out and explore the wonderful world of capitalism and consumerism. Here are several spending excuses to avoid that will help you keep more of your hard-earned money in your wallet, rather than in the retailer's cash register.

1. "I'll have the money by the time I have to pay off the loan, and that is why I want to buy it now." Don't buy it until you have the money in hand. That will allow you time to think about the purchase to determine if it is something you really need.

2. "I have to have it because this completes the set." We seem duty bound to match things we already have, even if we don't need or want them. Don't buy it just because it completes a set unless it is something that you use on a routine basis.

3. "I'm worth it, and therefore I deserve it." If you're about to buy something you have always wanted but don't need, forget it! The fact that you are worth it and deserve it doesn't answer the basic question. Do you really need it?

4. "The price is going up." Salespeople know that this old trick is one of the best ways to hook a tentative customer. Don't bite on the "going up" bait! Chances are it will be there tomorrow at the same or a lower price.

#57. How do I create a "spend-less" plan?

After you complete your budget, you should see some money-saving areas within your personal realm that you can tackle right away. Here are three simple steps to help you get started:

1. Identify what are necessary expenses and what are luxury expenses. For example, does each family member really need a cell phone? Do you truly need the most expensive cable television package?

2. Review your miscellaneous spending. Is there anything you can do away with? Do you see any patterns in your spending behavior that you can address?

3. Prioritize your budget. List your expenditures from the most important to the least important. Then assess what you can do away with or cut back on.

#58. What is the best way to get my family to participate in my spend-less plan?

Anyone who is spending part of your family's money has to be involved in your spend-less plan or it will probably fail. They can't support a plan they don't know about, so start by showing it to them. To grab their attention, state why you've created this plan. Don't sugarcoat your reasons. Tell them the truth: "It is absolutely essential that we reduce what we are all spending on a daily basis or we will destroy this family's financial future." After you have made your opening statement, wait patiently for a response before you proceed. If anyone doesn't understand the importance of what you're trying to tell them, start over again with a new or revised opening statement. Once you've got their attention, solicit their ideas and their participation in implementing the plan.

#59. What are some ways that I can cut back on gasoline for my car?

Here are several things you can do to improve your car's miles per gallon (MPG) to reduce what you're spending for gasoline by 15 percent or more:

Accelerate smoothly. Avoid sudden starts, which are hard on the engine and use more gas. When braking, take your foot off the accelerator well in advance of the stop sign or light to allow gravity to slow down your car. Racing to a stop sign so that you can jam on the brakes substantially reduces your MPG and wears out the brakes.

Check your owner's manual and use gasoline with the octane rating recommended by the manufacturer. Buying gas with higher octane than necessary is a waste of money.

Higher freeway speeds generally reduce MPG. Most cars get their best MPG at cruising speeds of 55 miles per hour. Anything beyond that reduces MPG. When you're cruising down a long hill or grade, take your foot off the accelerator and allow gravity to help move the car.

Keep your tires inflated at the proper pressure. Underinflated tires cause excessive tire wear and waste gasoline. Don't carry unneeded weight in your car. Excess weight puts an additional load on the engine and wastes gasoline.

Use your air conditioner only when it is needed. Air conditioners put an extra load on the engine and eat up extra gas. Keep your vehicle tuned. Dirty air cleaners, improper valve clearances, worn plugs, and dirty oil all contribute to poor gas mileage.

#60. I'm spending a lot of money each month on home energy bills. How can I cut back?

Utility bills can be a significant monthly expense. In many parts of the country, utility companies offer lower rates to customers who use their electric services during off-peak hours. Off-peak hours generally refer to hours that are outside of prime business hours when the demand for electricity is at its highest. By taking advantage of off-peak rates, you can significantly reduce your electric bill. Here are several additional ways to save on your utility bills:

Heating your home is one of your highest expenses during the winter months. Turn your heat down or off when nobody is home. Put on a sweater when you get home and turn the heat back on. Close the heat vents in any room that does not need to be heated. Make sure that pipes will not freeze in these areas, however. Use a space heater to heat the areas you use most in addition to your regular heat.

Cooling a home during the summer months is also an expensive proposition. Turn your air conditioner down or off when nobody is home, even if you leave the house for a short shopping trip. Close the AC vents in any room that does not need to be cooled. Use energy-efficient fans instead of air conditioning whenever possible.

#61. I'm considering refinancing my home. How should I do it?

Figure out why you want to refinance. Are you trying to lower your monthly payments? Or are you trying to pay off your home faster so that you can apply your mortgage payment to pay off your other debts? Your financial goal will help determine if you should refinance and what type of loan to get. Run the numbers. Shop for mortgage refinance loans that will give you a clearer idea of how much refinancing will cost you and then use a good web refinance calculator (such as *www.hsh.com/usnrcalc.html*) to help you determine if it's worthwhile.

#62. Is there any way I can reduce my monthly house payment without having to refinance?

If mortgage insurance is included in your monthly mortgage payment, get rid of it if you can. When you purchased your home, you had to carry mortgage insurance if you put down less than 20 percent of your home's purchase price. Mortgage insurance protects your lender (not you) in the event that you default on your mortgage, and it is expensive. It can cost you as much as $50 a month for every $100,000 you borrowed. If the value of your home is now 20 percent or more above what you owe on it through what you have paid on the principle and/or appreciation, you should aggressively try to get your lender to cancel mortgage insurance. It's a ripoff that lenders and insurance companies have known about for years. Now you too know about it.

In summary, there are two general conditions you must be able to meet to drop mortgage insurance, depending on the rules of your mortgage company: (1) your mortgage balance is less than 80 percent of what you paid for the house and (2) your mortgage balance is 75 percent or less of the current appraised value.

#63. I have accumulated $10,000 in credit card debt. What should I do?

The fact that you have accumulated $10,000 in credit card debt is not the real issue you need to address. What was your cumulative credit card debt six, three, and one month ago? If it has steadily increased, then you have a spending problem that you may be hiding under all those credit cards that you carry in your wallet. If, on the other hand, you have managed to reduce the balance of your credit cards over the last six months, congratulations. You are showing that you can pay off your credit cards because of your willpower to spend less.

#64. **I rent. What can I do to keep my rent from always going up?**

Being a renter can be very frustrating. Every time you turn around, you are plagued with an increase in rent. There are several things you can do that will help you keep your rent cost down. Rent from a private party whenever possible. If you rent from a corporation that owns the property and hires a property manager where everything is run by a computer, you are more likely to face automatic, periodic rent increases. If you rent from an individual who values you as a good renter, they may be less inclined to automatically increase your rent.

Get to know your landlord as a friend, rather than a bill collector. Landlording is a tough job, and if you can establish a solid relationship, he will be more likely to not increase your rent. Don't ask your landlord to do anything that you can do yourself, as long as it is within reason. If the sink or toilet is plugged, unplug it yourself. If a wall needs painting and the landlord has no problem with you painting it, do it yourself and then in a subtle way, let your landlord know how self-sufficient you are. He'll appreciate it. Always pay your rent on time. Landlords have bills to pay that are dependent upon getting their rent checks on time. Keep your place neat. Landlords like to rent to people who will take care of their property.

#65. **What are some ways to save when I shop for food?**

Anyone can lower grocery bills by using coupons from the Sunday paper, eating the leftovers in the refrigerator first before you go shopping, and cleaning out the pantry. But how do you establish a grocery shopping style that will allow you to consistently reduce your monthly grocery bill without sacrificing the foods your family enjoys? Here's how:

> **Plan your meals.** To reduce the temptation of going out to eat or ordering fast food, keep your pantry and freezer stocked with good, quick-fix meals. Buy bargain-priced in-season produce.

Check the offer against the regular price before you assume you're getting a deal. Make a list before you head to the grocery store of everything you need and then scan the store ads to find sales on any of your listed items. Don't buy nongrocery items like health or beauty products in a grocery store unless you know they are competitively priced.

Always check unit prices and container weights. Just because two identical items with different brands appear to be in the same size container does not mean that the weight of the food content is the same. Don't forget to give the cashier all of your coupons and check the register receipt to make sure you got credit for every coupon. Shop at more than one store and take advantage of their sales.

#66. Is it worth my while to try to reduce the interest rate I'm paying?

When you look at your monthly expenses, you will notice that many of the bills include the cost of interest (e.g., mortgages, car loans, credit cards). Call each lender and ask, "Can you lower the interest rate that I'm paying on your loan?" Some lenders are willing to refinance mortgages and car loans. With credit cards, you can transfer the balance on your current card to a cheaper card. If you tell your current card issuer that you're thinking of doing this, they may reduce your rate to avoid losing your account.

Chapter **8**

MAKING HARD CHOICES

Sometimes cutting back on what you're spending is all you need to do to get your financial life in order. If it doesn't make a big enough dent to help you make ends meet, you may need to look at some major items that are costing you the most money. You may have to make some hard choices now if you truly want to become debt free and financially independent. If you haven't been able to bring your expenses in line with what you make, the question is not whether you are going to have to make hard choices, but rather which hard choices you are going to take.

#67. What are some of the hard choices that I need to consider to get out of debt?

If your personal debt is escalating to the point where you can't even pay the minimum on your debts and collection agencies are hounding you, then you need to take some hard action right now. Consider:

1. Can I cut back on what I am paying for rent or mortgage payments until I get my debt under control? Will that necessitate a move?

2. My car expenses including the high price of gasoline are taking every spare dime I have. Should I get rid of my car and start using public transportation?

3. The interest rates that I am paying on my credit cards are so high. Do I really need to rely on credit cards?

4. I can't save any money to cover purchases so I just go deeper into debt. Should I just give up and declare bankruptcy?

#68. Who should I see who can help me decide what hard choices I need to make?

In the end, you probably are the one who will have to make final decisions about what you need to do to resolve your debt problems. However, that should not stop you from seeking the advice of anyone you can find who may have some viable ideas that may help. Immediate sources to consider are:

- Any and all family members who will be directly affected by any hard choice you're considering
- Personal friends and associates whom you can trust not to disclose your personal situation to others and who have personal finance expertise

Show whomever you're talking to a list of the choices you are considering and ask her for her opinion. Then sit back and listen to what she has to say.

#69. Should I consider selling my home?

Unfortunately, it may be that selling your home is a solution to your debt problem that you have to consider. It may be necessary to swap a larger house for a smaller, more affordable one, or rent for a while. If you're already renting, can you find a cheaper place to rent? Can you keep the cost of moving in line with what you will be saving? Would moving closer to work be more cost effective (i.e., cut transportation costs)?

#70. **Is my car sabotaging my ability to make ends meet?**

Is there a cheaper way for you to get back and forth to work each day? There probably is if you think about it. If you're willing to get rid of your car for a while, you could save the cost of its payments, upkeep, gasoline, and insurance. If you can't survive without a car, how about trading your car for a less expensive model that can get you from point A to point B just fine, with less luxury. This will also save you money on auto insurance. If you have an older car, you may not need expensive collision coverage.

#71. **Should I really consider getting rid of all my credit cards?**

Yes. The average credit card carries an interest rate of 18 percent or more. If you are making the minimum payment allowed on a credit card with a $1,000 balance, it will take you twelve years to pay it off. You might say, "How can I survive without my credit cards?" It's a big change, but you can do it. You don't need to close all your accounts. Leave one open in case you need to use it for emergency funds. Credit cards are covered in more detail in Chapter 13.

#72. **I am totally unable to save money. How can I change my ways?**

By not saving, you are forced to borrow anytime you need something that you didn't plan for. The itemized statement that you receive from your credit card company is probably loaded with unplanned items that you purchased last month. If your car broke down, you probably borrowed the money to get it repaired. And the list goes on.

If you don't have a savings account, you are going to put everything on your credit card, which increases your debt load. One of the most basic decisions you need to make is to open a savings account. That will take about ten minutes the next time you're at the bank. Now comes the hard part. Start depositing a set amount every month into your savings account, and at the end of three months, see if all the money you deposited is still in your savings. If it is, you are on your way to saving money. If it's not, you are back where you started from.

#73. I own some valuable assets that I don't need or want. How can I determine what to sell them for?

Whatever item you are considering selling, it is important to have an idea of its value before you sell it. If it's a motor vehicle, consult a guidebook like the Kelley Blue Book (*www.kbb.com*). If it's a piece of jewelry, get it appraised by a certified appraiser. If you are selling a household item that would be difficult to get an appraisal on, see what similar items are selling for in the classified advertisements or on *www.ebay.com*. Decide whether you want to sell your item yourself or through a broker. There are brokers listed online who are willing to sell just about anything for a fee.

#74. Should I consider bankruptcy to get out of debt, or are there alternatives?

There are alternatives to bankruptcy. Lenders may be willing to compromise their claim for a smaller cash payment or they may be willing to stretch payments out so you can pay their debts off over a longer period of time. You won't know what they are willing to do unless you make the contact. It costs you nothing to ask, and always remember that the last thing creditors want to do is to turn you over to a collection agency. They'll only get about half of whatever the agency collects. When *Smart Money* magazine called ten of the largest credit card issuers, posing as a distraught debtor, five agreed to reduce their interest rates.

However, an increasing number of people have run up six-figure debt on five-figure incomes. These people will never obtain an income level that will allow them to get out of debt. They are more likely to struggle for years trying to manage their personal finances and will never be able to pay off what they owe. The huge interest rates they're saddled with will compound the financial burden they are under as time goes on. If in your judgment there is no possibility of your getting out of debt, then you need to consider the option of bankruptcy.

If you need more information about bankruptcy, go to the website at *www.clearbankruptcy.com.*

#75. If I decide to declare bankruptcy, how do I apply?

To file, you draw up a plan to repay your existing debts, usually within a three-year period. Depending on your circumstances, your plan could show how you'll pay off your debts in full, or in part, where you pay only a percentage of every dollar you owe.

When you file, the court issues a restraining order stopping your creditors' collection efforts. If the court approves your payment plan, you'll make a single monthly payment to a court-appointed trustee who in turn pays your creditors. As long as you are under the plan, the court can exercise some control over your finances. For example, if you take on new debt, the court can immediately cancel the plan.

#76. How much does it cost to declare bankruptcy?

Most bankruptcies are performed using the services of an attorney. When you call a bankruptcy attorney, ask what the minimum charge is for a private individual's bankruptcy. If they tell you, "Well, that all depends," politely end the conversation and call the next attorney on your list. There are two points that we want to make here. First, bankruptcy is not a complicated legal procedure, so it is not unreasonable to ask for basic cost information. Second, attorney fees for bankruptcies can vary, so it pays to shop. It is possible for you to represent yourself in bankruptcy. If this approach interests you, get a how-to book on bankruptcy.

#77. Who can I consult to help me determine if I should declare bankruptcy?

The act of declaring bankruptcy is not something you want to openly share with anyone you don't trust. It should initially be shared with the people who are directly affected by the act of declaring bank-ruptcy. That includes your spouse, whose credit rating will be severely damaged just like yours. The only other people on your immediate list would be those who need to know what you are doing. If you decide to discuss the matter with a "don't need to know" person, make sure you have a good reason for doing so. For example, if this person can provide you with some information critical to making the decision, then contact him.

#78. **Do I need credit counseling and support?**

If you made it this far in the book and you still have no idea of what you need to do to get out of debt, consider getting help from a credit counselor. They put you on a "debt management program" or DMP. If you apply and they accept you as a client (you can be turned down if they don't believe you're serious), your counselor will arrange for you to pay off your debts usually at a lower interest rate. In exchange, you have to agree to stop using your credit cards and applying for additional credit. From this point on, you make one payment (usually monthly). If you need psychological support, you may be able to find a support group in your area. These are people just like you who are trying to get out of debt. Start your search on the Internet at *www.simpleliving.net.* There is also Debtors Anony-mous, which is a twelve-step program that's based on the same principles as Alcoholics Anonymous. Reach them at *www.debtors anonymous.org.*

PART 2

Finding Money

Chapter 9

PAYING YOURSELF FIRST

Now that you know more about your personal debt and how you can begin to manage it intelligently, you can begin to fine-tune your game plan. Getting rid of debt takes money. You should have identified several ways to come up with some of the money you'll need from the previous chapters that also addressed the subject. Now, what are you going to do with that money? Pay yourself first before you run out and spend it on something you don't need.

#79. What does "paying yourself first" mean?

When you get your paycheck, do you immediately deposit it so that you finally have some money in your pocket, and then pay off a bunch of bills to keep your creditors off your back? What you really need is a savings account that you can count on for emergency funds in between pay periods to meet those unexpected bills. You can only do this if you are willing to pay yourself first. Make up a savings "bill" in the form of a card or envelope labeled "savings bill" that you keep with your other monthly bills. When it comes time to pay the bills, make sure it's the first bill that gets paid and deposit the check you make out to yourself into your savings account.

If you discover that after you pay off all your bills you have some money left over, then make another deposit into your savings account. Deposit any coupon refund money or rebate checks you get directly into your savings account. Find out if your employer's payroll system allows you to make direct deposits into a savings account. If it does, sign up for a direct deposit tomorrow, and in a short time, you won't even miss the money that's deducted from your paycheck.

#80. Can I lower the amount of taxes that are withheld from my paycheck as a way of paying myself first?

If you get a tax refund every year, consider this option. Ask payroll to increase your personal deductions, which you are allowed to do (e.g., from one to two or three). The immediate result will be a lower income-withholding amount, resulting in a larger take-home paycheck for you. Instead of paying Uncle Sam first, you are now paying yourself first. But if you take this action, you may forfeit the tax return money you get at the end of the year.

#81. Where should I put the money that I pay myself?

You want that money someplace where you won't be tempted to spend it on something you don't need. You may decide to give it to your spouse or trusted friend because she has more self-control about spending money. Depositing it in an "out of the way" savings account (i.e., one that is not readily accessible) is another option. For example, you could elect to increase your payroll tax deductions, which will result in more of your income being withheld in state and federal taxes. That way you'll get a tax refund at the end of the year on money that would be difficult for you to access. The disadvantage of this system is that you won't earn any interest on the withheld money.

#82. Should I use the money I pay myself for savings or paying off debt first?

The question to save or repay first is one that people love to debate. The savers argue that the more cash you have on hand, the better you can survive a financial emergency without running up more debt. The payers will counterargue that most people are paying much higher interest on their debt than they're able to make in savings accounts. Therefore, it makes financial sense to pay off debts first.

Who's right? As you probably guessed, they're both right. Saving money is a learned art that requires a lot of discipline to make happen. We would urge you to save first, and then use a portion of what you have saved—say, 50 percent—to pay off your high-interest debts.

#83. What is a simple way of paying myself first?

Every morning before you go to work, rummage through your wallet and see if you can find a $5 bill or at least some amount of cash. Pay yourself the first thing every morning with that. Remove the bill(s) from your wallet and hide them in an out-of-the-way place. At the end of the week, you should have $25 that you can deposit into your savings account.

#84. Okay, I got the concept that's behind the paying-yourself-first idea. What are some things that I can do to make it a part of my daily plan?

These examples will help you get started:

Monday: Stop buying expensive mocha coffee and roll at Starbucks and pay yourself with the money you would have spent.

Tuesday: Turn the air conditioner up or the heat down five degrees before you leave for work and use the money you save on your utility bill to pay yourself.

Wednesday: Commute to work with one of your associates and use the money you save on gasoline to pay yourself.

Thursday: Stop buying expensive frozen foods and use the money you save to pay yourself.

Friday: Stop going out to lunch with buddies; take a sandwich to work instead, and pay yourself with the money saved.

#85. **As soon as I pay myself, I spend the money. What can I do?**

Then stop paying yourself and pay someone else you trust with your money. That could be your spouse, relative, or trusted friend. Just make sure that whomever you select knows what you're trying to accomplish. There are lots of books available at the local library that address overspending. Read them all.

#86. **Why are you making a big deal out of the pay-yourself-first exercises?**

If you can't figure out a way to pay one of the most important people you know (i.e., yourself) first, then you will have difficulty resetting your debt priorities. If this were a weight loss plan, one of your first steps would be to figure out how much weight you want to lose and by when. Perhaps your answer is ten pounds over the next two months. That means you need to lose about a pound a week.

Think about your pay-yourself plan the same way. Let's suppose you need to pay back $1,000 on your credit card. If you can figure out a way of paying yourself $100 a month, you can pay off the card in ten months. Once you settle on the debt diet that is right for you, do it!

Chapter **10**

SEARCHING FOR HIDDEN MONEY

Unfortunately, it takes money to get out of debt—and in many cases, it takes a lot of money. The previous chapter discussed several ways you could pay yourself first to come up with some extra cash for your savings account. Most of the money-saving options that were identified were relatively easy to implement. Now it is time to address some tougher areas for you to find the additional money you may need.

#87. Where do I start my search to find hidden money?

Figure out a way to spend less. Okay, you already knew that, but it is a basic philosophy that underlies the theme of this chapter and worth repeating. We spend money on things we need, like medical care. But we also spend money on things we want but don't need, like that fancy SUV. You can't do much about the "need" part of your spending plan, but there is a lot you can do to reduce the "want" part of your spending if you are willing to address it. Get rid of all your wants until you're debt free. Then, buy your wants with cash rather than with credit.

#88. **What are five sources of money that I should look at first?**

Although you may not buy into all of the saving ideas covered in this chapter, if you implemented just a couple, you could save $100 or more per month. And these ideas should trigger thoughts about additional ways to save money. For every idea listed, you should be able to come up with at least two or more of your own. Do whatever it takes to come up with at least $100 and then hang onto the money. Here are five sources of money to consider:

1. Charge nothing for the next thirty days and add up the interest you save.
2. Buy generic brand foods whenever possible. Shop with a list and stick to it to help you avoid impulse buying. Buy generic drugs any chance you get. Purchase only sale items.
3. Make sure your car is running as efficiently as possible by getting a tune-up, properly inflating the tires, and using the least expensive gas with the proper octane rating.
4. Stop subscribing to magazines you don't read. Rent a DVD instead of going to the movies. Look for cheap and often better entertainment options like museums, zoos, a walk in the park, or picnics with friends. Start using your local library, which is free.
5. Buy gifts that are on sale for major holidays like Christmas and birthdays. Limit your spending to a specific amount. Remember, it is the thought that counts.

#89. **I have a friend who keeps telling me that buying used is better than buying new. Do you agree?**

We all have great stories about something that we bought used for a "fantastic" bargain price, perhaps at a garage sale. The rapid expansion of eBay attests to the national infatuation of buying used. And who can really argue the point? For example, a new Sony widescreen television that sells for $1,000 can routinely be purchased on eBay for $500 or less. Consider buying used any chance you get to save money.

#90. **I'm responsible for paying back student loans that cost me a lot each month. What can I do to reduce my monthly loan payments?**

Try consolidating your student loans, which could free up a considerable amount of cash. If you took out your loans when interest rates were higher, you have an opportunity to roll all of those loans over into one loan at a lower interest rate. How do you do it? If all of your loans are through a single lender, then it is probably easier to work with them to consolidate. If you got loans through several lenders, call each one and ask what they can do to help you consolidate. If you enter "student loan consolidation" into any web browser, you will get a long list of companies anxious to help you consolidate. Before you sign up, check each carefully for excessive loan fees, high interest rates, and the lack of prepayment options.

#91. **Should I consider getting a cheaper car?**

Next to the overuse of credit cards, the automobile is the biggest cause of people falling into debt. The actual cost of a car and subsequent car payments is just the tip of the iceberg. License fees, insurance, and maintenance can easily cost several hundred dollars a month. A trip to the gas station that used to cost $50 for a tank of gas has more than doubled. If you are supporting two cars, try to get by on one. If you have a relatively new car, you would be better off with a cheaper used car that gets better mileage.

#92. **My monthly car payment is a killer. What can I do to bring it down to earth?**

Most people don't know that it is easier to refinance a car loan than it is to refinance a mortgage. And, there are several advantages. There are no appraisal fees, and finance fees are usually minimal. If this option interests you, make sure you first know what your car is worth by consulting the Kelly Blue Book at the library or on the web at *www.kbb.com*. If it is worth more than you owe, you are in good shape. If it is not, then the only option you have is asking your lender if they will either reduce the interest rate or extend the payment terms. If you have equity in your car, shop around for a better loan. The best car loans are usually offered by credit unions and online lenders. Bankrate.com is an excellent site with a search engine that can find the best rates nationally and in your area.

#93. What are equity lines, and are they a viable source of money?

Equity lines of credit combine the best features of mortgage loans and revolving credit. The asset (i.e., your home) secures the loan, so interest rates are far lower than unsecured credit loans. The time periods of equity loans are defined but are usually long term, like five to ten years, with regular payment periods. Interest is usually tax deductible. Equity loans can work well if the money is used to retire debt as opposed to acquiring unneeded stuff.

#94. How much money do I need to find to get out of debt?

The answer will be based on how much you need to pay off all your debts, either in a lump sum or in a single monthly payment that you can afford. Let's suppose that you need $10,000 in a lump sum to pay off all your debts (excluding home mortgage) or an additional $200 a month to pay off the same debts in five years. As you proceed through the questions in this chapter, you may discover ways to immediately free up some cash to pay off certain debts and ways to refinance part of your debt load. Suppose you were only able to find enough money to cover just a portion of your debts. It's a start, so be positive and move on to the next step.

#95. How can I keep myself motivated to keep looking for money to get out of debt?

Find a quiet location where you can be by yourself, sit back, close your eyes, and think. What would your life be like if you were debt free? How would it change your life? Would you be happier? What about your relationships with the people you really care about? If the out-of-debt vision that you create is something that you both want and need, make it the foundation of your drive to get out of debt. Make sure everything you do supports your vision.

#96. There have got to be ways to reduce what I'm paying for insurance. Can you help me find some hidden money in my insurance premiums?

One of the best places to look for hidden money is on the itemized statement that identifies what you're paying for the deductibles on your policies. Homeowners policies typically have a deductible amount that is associated with the theft and repair portions of the policy. A deductible of $250, $500, $1,000, or higher is quoted on the policy statement. What that means is that if you have a theft or suffer insurable damage to your home, you are responsible for paying the deductible before your insurance pays the balance. The higher the deductible, the lower the insurance premium. The same principle applies to the deductible on your auto policy, which also covers theft and damage. The deductible option can be one of the most expensive components of insurance premiums. For example, the premium difference between a $500 and $250 deductible may be $100 annually. That means if you were to increase your deductible from $250 to $500, you would save $100. You are paying $100 to insure $250, which is not a good deal. Check what your insurance deductibles are and how much you could save if you increased the amount.

#97. Do I need to keep track of everything I'm doing to find money?

Yes, because you need to monitor which strategies work and which don't. So record in writing everything you do to find the money you need to get out of debt. This will tell you a lot about how you're doing. When you hit a winner that gives you cash, the reward of knowing that you're doing something right will motivate you to continue your search. If you hit a foul ball, do not despair. Analyze what you did wrong so that you can hit a winner the next time around. Consider the following statistics from *Money* magazine:

Eighty-five percent of the people who are in debt believe that no matter how much money they make, they will always be able to live on it.

Over half of those people can't pay off their credit cards each month and are saving nothing.

Most people refuse to live on whatever they make. By over-spending, not saving, and refusing to keep track of where they are financially, they will never get out of debt.

Chapter **11**

USING HOME EQUITY

Home equity is the difference between what your home is worth on the open market and what you owe on it. You don't want to squander a loan on a long-term asset to accommodate short-term spending. Using your home equity for items like vacations, big-screen TVs, and credit card payments is foolish. The intent of this chapter is to give you a better appreciation for what home equity is and why it is an essential part of your financial well-being.

#98. I have a lot of equity in my home. Should I keep my house or sell it?

If you bought your home years ago, chances are you've ended up with an asset that's worth more than what you paid for it. Over the past three decades, the rise in single-family home prices has become the cornerstone of many Americans' retirement nest egg. The opportunity to leverage the equity they've built up in their homes has become the foundation of their retirement plan. As you approach retirement, there are several options to consider when you evaluate whether you should keep or sell your home:

Consider trading down. Estimate your profit before you consider selling. What will it cost for an acceptable replacement?

If the potential profit from selling your home is minimal, it might not be worth the effort of trading down.

Time the sale of your home to take advantage of tax breaks. If you or your spouse is fifty-five or older, you can exclude from taxes up to $500,000 of the capital gains on the sale of your home.

Consider keeping your home and refinancing it with an individual reverse mortgage (IRM) or a leaseback. In this arrangement, a lender receives part or all of the equity in your home, in return for payments that you receive for the rest of your life. Make sure you know the pros and cons before signing this kind of contract.

Sell your home and move to a part of the country where the cost of housing and living are lower. Not only will you get more home for your money, you will also get the added benefit of a lower cost of living in the new area.

#99. Is a reverse mortgage an option that I should consider?

A reverse mortgage allows you to borrow back the equity in your principal residence. As you once paid the bank to build up the equity in your home, some banks are willing to repay you some of your equity and allow you to stay in your home. In most cases, you have to be sixty-two or older to qualify for a reverse mortgage. The amount that you can borrow depends on your age, the value of your home, and the current interest rate. And the loan doesn't have to be paid until you sell your home or die. If you take a reverse mortgage loan, you can elect to get your payout in several ways: as a line of credit, a monthly payment, a lump sum, or some combination of the three.

#100. Who makes home equity loans, and what are the costs and risks?

Savings and loan associations and banks are the primary sources for home equity loans. You typically can get a lower interest rate on an equity loan than you can on just about any other loan.

Home equity loans are not inexpensive to set up, however. In most cases, you will be charged an appraisal fee for your home and loan origination fees that will cost you several hundred dollars. Make sure these fees are disclosed to you before you enter into any loan agreement. Equity loans are typically from five to fifteen years in duration and therefore require a higher monthly payment than a thirty-year mortgage.

Be aware that by borrowing against the equity in your home, you may be leveraging the most valuable asset you have in your portfolio. The risks can therefore be significant. Using up all the equity in your home in a fast-rising real estate market poses several problems, as we recently witnessed in the subprime fiasco. Hot markets can suddenly cool, dropping the average home value. If you have used up all of the equity and need to relocate, you may be forced to sell your home for less than what you owe on it. And if you fail to make your equity loan payments, the lending institution can foreclose on your home.

#101. When does it make sense to consider a home equity loan?

A home is a source of wealth for many people, and its equity should not be used on something that is of a lesser value, like a luxury car. NEVER use home equity to cover expenses like vacations or weddings, or for buying big-ticket items like a new car. Using the equity in your home to pay off high-interest debts may make sense if you have proven to yourself that you will not run up more debt once your old debt is paid off. There are advantages to using home equity financing to pay off other debts. Interest rates are often much lower than debt rates and the interest on an equity loan is tax deductible.

#102. Should I borrow against the equity in my home to finance college for my kids?

Yes. Your kids deserve a college education that will pay them back many times over in their future earnings. College loans that are backed by equity are relatively easy to get at attractive interest rates. However, there are several viable alternative ways to fund college expenses that should be explored before you tap into your equity. Search the Internet to get a preview of what is available. There are a number of federal and state agencies that offer financial aid. Almost every college offers aid. There are thousands of scholarships that are also available for any student who is willing to step forward and ask for one. Financial aid for college is covered in detail in the next chapter.

#103. My friends tell me that there are a number of financial benefits that are attached to home equity. What are they?

Buying a home to live in not only provides needed shelter but it can help you financially. Here's how:

> **Forced savings.** Instead of paying rent that goes nowhere, you are paying into a home that you will someday own.

> **Tax deductions.** The interest on your mortgage and property taxes is one of the few remaining tax shelters for most people.

> **Appreciation.** As real estate prices appreciate over time, your home should be worth more than you paid for it.

#104. What questions should I ask myself before I take out a home equity loan?

Whenever you're tempted to use your home equity, ask yourself how important the purchase you will use the money for is. Will it help you or a family member achieve a significant goal in life, like getting out of debt or continuing your or their education? Will you be buying something that won't appreciate in value? Are you willing to give up something that appreciates in value (equity in your home) for something that depreciates in value (car, furniture, etc.)? Are you willing to use something that you need (home) to obtain something that you want, like a vacation?

#105. Should I sell my home, use the equity to pay off debt, and rent or buy a cheaper home?

If you are heavily in debt, selling your home and finding a cheaper place to live may be one of your few remaining options. If your present house is eating up too much of your income, you have two choices:

1. Trade down to something cheaper.
2. Rent and use the equity from the sale of your home to pay off debt.

To figure out which way you should go, estimate the net sum of money you would have after the sale of your home. Then make the following comparisons:

If you use the equity from the sale of your home to pay off debt, how much more would you have at the end of the month in disposable income? Would you have enough to rent a place that would be acceptable to you?

If you use the equity from the sale of your home to purchase a less expensive home, how much would you save on your current monthly mortgage payment? Is the amount that you would save enough to make the move worth your while? Will you be able to use the money you save to substantially reduce your debts?

#106. **Why is it wise to repay equity loans on time and without fail?**

If you are late in your payments or fail to make an equity loan payment, your lender has the legal right to foreclose on your home. Miss one payment and you will receive by certified mail a "breach letter" from your lender advising you of your contract violation. You will be given thirty days to respond. If you don't respond, that letter serves as the right of the lender to foreclose and take over ownership of your home. Do not even think about taking out a home equity loan if there is any doubt in your mind that you won't be able to pay it back.

#107. **How does home equity fit into my retirement plan?**

When you retire, you want an easy lifestyle that you can afford. If you own your home at the time you retire, you will be able to "lock down" a significant part of your living expense. Mortgages typically cost the average household 25 percent or more of their monthly gross income. If you own 100 percent of your home when you retire (i.e., make no mortgage payments), a major part of what it will cost you to live will be covered.

Chapter **12**

PAYING COLLEGE EXPENSES

The cost of college continues to move into the stratosphere. Figuring out a way to pay for their child's college education is difficult for many parents. Fortunately, financial aid is available to millions of American families. Don't make the mistake of assuming you don't qualify. You won't know until you apply. There are thousands of financial aid sources for the people who are willing to search them out.

#108. I have a child who wants to go to college. How can I determine what it will cost?

First determine which college(s) your child wants to attend. Visit its website or call its administrative office and ask for a brochure that lists its average annual attendance costs. This shows what it would cost if your child were to attend that college today. Because the College Board estimates that college costs will increase by 7 percent or 8 percent per year over the next ten years, you can approximate what tuition will be when your child is ready to attend.

#109. Are there some tax-free ways to save for college?

The Taxpayer Relief Act of 1997 expanded eligibility for traditional IRAs and created a new Education IRA to help pay for college expenses. Although this savings vehicle is called an IRA, it has nothing to do with retirement planning. An Education IRA is a savings account for a child's future educational expenses. You can contribute up to $500 a year to an education fund for any child under the age of eighteen as long as your income does not exceed $95,000 for singles and $150,000 for married couples. Contributions to an Education IRA do not affect your personal IRAs.

Although the contributions are not tax deductible, the earnings are allowed to grow tax free. When your child finishes high school and moves on to a college or qualified training school, the Education IRA can be tapped to pay for school expenses. If the recipient reaches age thirty and chooses not to use the funds for educational purposes, the earnings are taxed and subject to a 10 percent penalty. The taxes and penalty can be avoided if the account is rolled over to another child.

#110. Are there preferred loans available to help me pay for my child's college?

Federal student loans are one way to pay for college. Loans must be repaid with interest, but have options for deferment and favorable repayment terms that typically do not start until after graduation. These loans generally have low interest rates and are not based on your credit history. Many schools are now participating in the federal Direct Loan Program where the schools rather than banks act as the lending institution and the federal government supplies the funds.

Both subsidized and unsubsidized Stafford loans are available through both the Federal Family Education Loan Program and the federal Direct Loan Program. The federal government pays the interest accrued on a subsidized Stafford loan until a student graduates. Federal Perkins loans are campus-based loans offering a low interest rate and are available to undergraduate and graduate students who have financial need. The school acts as the lender but uses partial funds from the federal government to cover the funding of the loan.

#111. What exactly is college financial aid and how can I apply?

There are three types of financial aid packages: scholarships or grants, loans, and campus jobs. Most of the aid is made available through the U.S. Department of Education (*www.usdoe.com*). Most of the federal aid is available through grant programs where you are awarded "free" money to apply toward tuition. Pell Grants are need-based grants funded by the federal government worth up to $2,340. Supplemental Education Opportunity Grants are campus-based federal grants that are based on financial need and award up to $4,000 per year. Eligible students must be an undergraduate to receive a Pell Grant.

Go where the money is. State schools generally have a higher amount of subsidies than private schools. However, some private schools have huge endowments, so they are worth checking out as well. Before your child decides exactly where she wants to go, find out how much each of the colleges under consideration has available in its grant fund by contacting its financial aid office. Your preference for a specific college may suddenly change once you find out what aid packages are available. Your eligibility for financial aid largely depends on your income at the time your child is actually attending college.

#112. How can I determine if I qualify for financial aid?

Your Expected Family Contribution (EFC), the amount of money you'll be expected to pay for your child's education, is key to the aid process. Colleges figure your EFC by applying a financial aid formula that takes into account your income, family size, marital status, age, personal assets, and any special circumstances, like high medical expenses you've recently had to pay. The amount of money you save for your child's education will affect your EFC. Once a college has calculated your EFC, it's compared to the college's cost of attendance. If your EFC is less than the attendance costs, you're eligible for financial aid. Question 113 gives the basic steps you go through to apply for aid.

#113. **How do I apply for federal college financial aid?**

Call the U.S. Department of Education (800-433-3243) and ask them to send you the Free Application for Federal Student Aid (FAFSA), or complete the application online at *www.fafsa.ed.gov*. Study the application to become familiar with the questions you'll be required to answer. For example, 401(k) plans or pension plans don't count as part of your current assets, so don't list them. If you do, it will reduce the amount of aid that you're eligible to receive. As a general rule, approximately 6 percent of your assets and up to 50 percent of your income will be considered available for college expenses. Always keep those percentages in mind when you fill out the application.

#114. **Who can help me learn more about financial aid?**

There is a small but growing number of financial consultants who can help you get through the process. Beware of the consultant who is more interested in selling you a financial product than helping you get the best aid package possible. Many charge fees for an in-depth aid eligibility analysis and their assistance in completing the application. Contact other parents they have successfully helped before you use their services. If a consultant can help increase your child's aid eligibility, then you should have no objections to paying his fee. Many community colleges have financial aid seminars at the beginning of the semesters, so check their program schedules.

#115. Do the individual colleges and state governments offer financial aid?

Most colleges have their own financial aid application forms that supplement the federal application. Ask the Financial Aid office of the colleges that your child is interested in to send you their form. Most of the information duplicates the federal form, but you should carefully read each of the questions anyway. Although the federal government doesn't count the equity you have in your home as an asset, most colleges do.

State funds for financial aid are also available and vary widely between the states, so contact your state's education department to learn more. School aid is also available directly from colleges in the form of need-based and non-need-based grants. The amount of financial assistance provided to you by a college will depend on the individual school's policies. Contact the financial aid offices of your child's preferred colleges to learn more.

#116. Where are the best places to find college scholarships?

Private sources for scholarships come from community associations, businesses, interest groups, and other organizations. Funds from these sources generally come in the form of scholarships or loans. Many employers help put students through college by means of cooperative education programs or work-study programs. Students alternate school semesters with work semesters or work part-time during the school year. Not only does this provide for a chance to build your child's professional skills, but it also helps finance her education. Many scholarship opportunities and applications can be found online. Also, check out Dave Rye's book *The Complete Idiot's Guide to College Financial Aid* for further information about scholarships.

#117. Are there ways to pay for college on an installment plan?

The amount of money you need to come up with at the start of the college school year can be staggering. Progressive colleges recognize the difficulties of this situation, and many now offer installment payment plans. You have the option of making monthly installment payments that typically cover tuition, room, and board over ten or twelve months. Most installment plans are interest free, although you may be charged a nominal annual administrative fee to enroll in the plan. Contact the college admissions office to find out if they have an installment plan.

Chapter **13**

CONTROLLING CREDIT CARDS

When consumer credit cards first came out in the early seventies, they were considered a status symbol. Your status increased in direct proportion to the number of cards you had. Today, over 50 million credit card charges are made every day, averaging $80 a transaction. Credit cards are the high-octane fuel that is powering the debt over-load in today's economy. Paying with cash like our parents used to do is not in our DNA anymore. We replaced cash with a plastic card.

#118. What's the difference between a debit card and a credit card?

They look the same but they have different effects on your overall debt. When you apply a purchase against a debit card, you are imme-diately paying electronically from funds that are linked to the card, like your checking account. You are in effect paying cash for the purchased item(s) and are incurring no additional debt. It's easier than writing out a check. With a credit card, the sponsor of the card (usually a bank) pays for the purchases you made against the card. You pay the card company back with interest at a later date. Debit card spending is limited to the on-hand balance in your checking account, while credit card spending is limited to your credit limit.

#119. **What is the primary purpose of credit cards?**

Credit cards provide financial protection that isn't easily available from other sources. The credit card company serves as a middleman if you have a dispute with a merchant. They can be used as a ready source of emergency funds if your car breaks down in an out-of-the-way place. And they are essential if you want to secure a purchase that you're trying to make on the Internet or telephone (e.g., airline tickets, hotel room). Credit cards are therefore ideally suited for making short-term purchases (i.e., purchases that you can pay off in one to two months). Long-term debts do not belong on your credit card.

#120. **What are the different types of credit cards and hidden costs of using them?**

Debit cards extract the money for whatever you just purchased from your checking or savings account, depending on the account you have designated.

Gold and platinum cards offer preferential services like product warranties and theft insurance. They also charge more for annual fees.

Reward credit cards offer you an incentive for their use like a discount at specified retail outlets.

Affiliate credit cards like Amazon.com's Visa Card offers discounts off their Internet product line.

Charge cards like American Express work like a credit card but require the balance to be paid off monthly.

Specialty credit cards are typically issued by department stores and oil companies. They can be useful for taking advantage of special company-sponsored sales.

The high interest rates are the hidden costs of using credit cards. For example, if you pay a $20 monthly minimum on a $1,000 credit card that charges 18 percent interest, it'll take you ninety-four months (seven and a half years) to pay the loan off. If you increased the payments to $40 a month, you'll pay the loan off in just thirty-four months (less than three years).

#121. What are the different types of fees charged by credit cards, and which one is best for me?

There are several different fee structures used by credit card companies. Some have lower interest rates but charge an annual fee. Other varieties offer competitive interest rates but vary in their bonus features. The best way to find out all the options and possibly the best one for you is at *www.e-wisdom.com*. This site offers personalized recommendations, based on information you supply, and shows comparison charts so that you can see the differences between all the cards offered. You may also choose to look at *www.card ratings.com*, which offers a variety of resources to help you understand everything related to credit cards.

#122. How do people get into trouble using credit cards?

Using credit cards is too easy! All you have to do is pull that magic plastic card out of your wallet, hand it to the cashier, and with one swipe you become the instant owner of something. You don't even have to think about how you're going to pay for it until you get your credit card statement in another month. Your initial shock at the total balance that's due on the statement turns into a smile when you look at the small minimum payment due. Getting too many credit cards and chasing lower interest rates by transferring balances from card to card compounds the credit card debt problem. Many people become focused on the rate rather than the balance.

#123. How can I motivate myself to limit what I'm charging to credit cards?

There's a limit to the amount of credit you can get on any one of your cards. If you have many credit accounts, the total limit available to you may be more than you can handle. So it's up to you to establish the credit limit that you can realistically handle. The first step is to determine what your personal credit limit should be by figuring out how much you can afford to pay each month for credit purchases. Once you establish your personal credit limit, plan your credit spending so that your total payments cover, at a minimum, your credit purchases plus interest. Record everything you charge in a memo book so you know where you are at any time during the month. You may be able to do this step online by viewing your account activities on your card's website.

#124. **What are some general guidelines for paying off credit cards?**

There are three approaches for you to consider. Pick the one that best fits your situation:

1. Pay off the smallest balance first. This approach quickly rewards you with achieving a zero balance on at least one of your accounts, a victory that will encourage you to continue your payoff plan. But if your other card debts are accruing at higher interest rates, you could end up paying more in total interest.
2. Pay off the highest rate first. (As mentioned earlier, there may be exceptions to this rule.) This is perhaps the most practical plan since it is designed to eliminate your costliest accounts first. However, it may take you longer to achieve if it has a high balance due.
3. Pay off the balance that is closest to its limit. If your card is maxed out, lenders can use that as an excuse to raise your interest rate. Paying off these high-balance cards can help you improve your credit score and ultimately reduce your total interest costs.

#125. **I'm charging everything to my credit cards. How do I just kick the habit for good?**

Kicking the credit card habit is a lot like kicking smoking. Hiding them in a safe place won't cut it. Take all of the credit cards out of your wallet, stack them neatly in a pile, and cut up all of them except for one to be used for emergencies only. If you are not able to accomplish this first step, you will never cure your credit card habit. Replace your credit cards with a debit card. If you don't have a debit card, visit the bank where you have a checking account and they will give you one. Start paying with either a debit card or check. Tell your family and close associates what you are doing and solicit their advice and encouragement.

#126. What will happen to me once I solve my credit card habit?

Three wonderful things that will happen. First, you'll start buying less of what you really don't need. When you use a credit card for a purchase, it doesn't feel the same as when you have to pull hard-earned money out of your wallet. According to recent studies, credit cards account for over 50 percent of the impulse-buying patterns of shoppers. Second, your total debt will start to shrink exponentially. As high-interest card balances get paid off, you'll end up with money you didn't know you had for investing or to pay off other loans. Finally, once you're out of debt, you'll feel great. Yes, you may keep one or two cards for emergency expenses to cover yourself. But when you learn to consistently pay the balance off at the end of each month, you will know you've kicked the credit card habit for good. Remember for every month you miss making a minimum balance payment, thirty or more points can get deducted from your credit score (refer to Question 43 for more information).

Chapter **14**

AVOIDING BAD LOANS

High-rate loans were once the province of loan sharks and pawnbrokers. Not anymore. Today, high-rate loans are big business. Most of the big banks now make payday loans, tax preparers push refund anticipation loans, and rent-to-own retail outlets offering excessive interest rate loans are in every major city in the country. They all capitalize on people's desire for quick cash, regardless of the cost. Although many of these loans target low-income working people who may feel they have limited options, the promotion schemes are getting more sophisticated and attracting higher-income people.

#127. Is there any such thing as a good loan?

Throughout, this book implies that all debt is bad and that the less you have, the better off you'll be. However, some debt can do good things to your financial future. For example, a mortgage used to acquire a home provides you with a place to live in an asset that historically increases in value. The interest on home mortgages is tax deductible. An educational loan can boost your (or your kids') income over time. Good debt offers you a favorable return on whatever it is you are financing. Conversely, bad debt does not offer you a favorable return. If you use it to support excessive spending on something that depreciates in value, think twice before you do it.

#128. What are the symptoms of a bad loan?

A bad loan has interest rates that exceed the prevailing rates by 20 percent or more and loan terms that include unreasonable late payment penalties, prepayment penalties, or loan costs. Bad becomes worse if you have saddled yourself with payments that you're struggling to meet each month. Ninety percent of the ownership of taking on a bad loan rests with the borrower, not the lender. Lenders may entice you with their ads and twisted words to con you into accepting a loan that's bad for you, but in the end you make the decision.

#129. What are the three basic types of loans, and what are the advantages and disadvantages of each type?

1. Revolving credit loans allow you to borrow up to a predetermined limit for a defined period of time (e.g., one to five years). The advantage is that these loans are convenient in that you can use them whenever you need money. They charge a stiff interest rate for this convenience.
2. Installment loans are fixed loan amounts over a specified period of time at a fixed interest rate. They are used to finance large purchases like cars, which are used as collateral for the loan. Therefore, they typically carry a lower interest rate than other loans.
3. Line of credit loans are secured by an asset (e.g., your home) and therefore charged lower interest rates than the other loan options. Your credit limit is set and you are issued a checkbook when the loan is approved. You can write a check against your credit limit whenever you want.

#130. How do I determine if I have any bad loans?

List on a sheet of paper each of your loans, how much you owe, the minimum monthly payment you're allowed to make, and the gross interest rate you are paying. Note the amount of any penalty fees you are charged for late payments. Based upon what you are now paying on a monthly basis, determine when the loan will be paid off. If you need help making that determination, go to the website *www.calculators.usatoday.com* for assistance. With the exception of mortgage debts, any debt that will take you in excess of five years to pay off qualifies as a potential bad loan.

#131. **What are some of the loans that I should avoid at all costs?**

Payday loans. These are short-term loans that you get before your payday. Let's say you need $200 ten days before your payday. To accommodate your need, a lender will loan you the $200 for a fee of, say, $10. You write a postdated check for the $200 and you are happy. You just paid the lender the equivalent of 260 percent interest, annualized.

Direct deposit advances. If your paycheck is deposited directly into your checking account, your bank may offer direct deposit loans. They charge a set amount for every dollar amount you borrow. For example, a $2 charge for every $20 borrowed is not uncommon. The annualized interest exceeds 100 percent in most of these types of loans.

Pawn shop loans. These make loans on an item that you give them for collateral. As a rule of thumb, pawn shops will loan you about 25 percent of what they consider is the retail value of the item. If you don't repay the loan by a specified date, the shop can sell the item and keep all of the proceeds from the sale.

#132. **What questions should I always ask a lender before I sign the loan papers?**

Don't limit yourself to asking just the questions listed here before you sign loan papers. Ask as many questions as you deem necessary to determine if you should accept the loan. The purpose of these sample questions is to point you in the right direction.

1. What was my credit score and which agency did you get it from?
2. Are there any prepayment penalties, and if so, what are they?
3. What happens if I am late in making a payment?
4. What interest rate will I be charged and how did you arrive at that rate?
5. Are there any conditions within the loan contract that I should particularly be aware of?

#133. Why should I avoid loans with prepayment penalties?

Prepayment penalties are stipulated in the loan papers that you sign and specify the fee (penalty) you will be required to pay if you decide to pay off your loan before it is due. Always ask if there is a prepayment penalty before you sign. If there is, read and understand the terms of the penalty. Why would a lender want to charge you additional money to pay off their loan? Because they want to avoid losing your lucrative business. By charging a prepayment penalty, the lender insures that they make a minimum profit on the loan, even if they don't receive all the interest over the original term. If you elect to pay them their prepayment penalty, the lender still wins. You may say "so what?" because you have no intention of prepaying any loan. But over time, that may change if it is to your financial advantage to pay off a loan.

#134. Is a loan against my retirement account a good idea?

It depends. You may be allowed to borrow part of the balance in your retirement account as a loan to yourself with strict stipulations. In most cases, you must repay yourself (i.e., your retirement account) within sixty days from when you withdrew the funds to avoid serious tax penalties. Before you exercise this option, discuss the rules with a person in the organization that administers your retirement plan. Retirement account loans are meant to satisfy short-term needs for cash. Since there is no cost for the loan, they can be used to meet your short-term cash requirements or buy you some time to shop for a long-term loan. Keep in mind that if you fail to pay it back in the allotted time, you will be required to pay stiff tax penalties on the money you withdrew, which is not negotiable with the IRS.

#135. **How does my credit score affect the cost of a loan?**

Let's say you borrowed $10,000 for five years when the prime rate (interest rate charged to customers with high credit scores) was 5 percent. What would that loan have cost you based on your credit score? The following table dramatically illustrates how much more you will have to pay if your credit score is low:

Cost of $10,000 Loan

Credit Score	Interest Rate	Annual Interest Payment	Total Interest Paid over Five Years
720–800	6%	$620	$1,500
700–719	7%	$725	$1,750
675–699	8%	$825	$2,000
620–674	10%	$1,035	$2,500
560–619	14%	$1,445	$3,500
Below 560	18%	$1,860	$4,500

#136. **What does a lender mean when they say you're "upside down" in your car loan?**

It means that you owe more than your car is worth, which puts you at serious financial risk. For starters, it prevents you from refinancing the loan on your car. If your car is stolen or totaled, you could find yourself owing money on a car you don't have. If for some reason you have to sell it for less than what you owe, you still have car payment debts hanging over you. There is a type of insurance called guaranteed auto protection that can cover the gap if your car gets stolen or totaled if you are upside down.

#137. How can I avoid getting a car loan that I can't afford?

What can you comfortably afford to pay on a monthly basis for a car loan? Don't buy a car if you are upside down (see Question 136) in your current car. Pay it off first. When you take out a loan, determine how long you plan to keep the new car and make sure the term of your loan does not exceed that or you will be upside down in the car you're buying. Know what your credit score is and what interest rate you're entitled to. Auto loans are strongly driven by scores, so make sure you don't get stuck with a more expensive loan.

#138. What alternatives do I have to avoid short-term high-rate loans?

If you owe money to a creditor now but won't have the money until payday, negotiate with them. You may be pleasantly surprised at how easy it is to get them to accommodate your payment delay. If you still need a short-term loan, talk to your credit union or local community bank. Their rates and terms may be substantially better than the big national banks.

Chapter 15

PAYING OFF DEBT

Some financial advisors will encourage you to pay off the smaller debts first regardless of interest rates to reduce your number of debts faster. Others say you should accept a multicard balance transfer offer and start paying on the one card while you still have access to credit on the "paid off" cards. The credit card consolidation option opens you up to the temptation of adding more debt to the very cards that got you into trouble in the first place. Both approaches are wrong. However, it makes financial sense to pay off your highest interest rates first because those are the ones that are costing you the most.

#139. How do I determine which debts I should pay off first?

Organize your outstanding loans from the highest to the lowest interest rate. If possible, increase the amount of your payments against your high interest rate loans first to get them paid off. A consolidation loan may be what you need at a lower interest rate to get out from under high interest rate debt. It may be smart to take out a home equity loan at a lower interest rate to pay them off. Borrow creatively at low rates to pay off high-interest loans. Many insurance companies offer low interest rate loans to their customers who have cash value in their life insurance policies. If you have a

401(k) retirement plan, check with your employer to see if you can borrow money against your plan (see Question 134).

#140. What payoff solutions should I avoid?

One type of payoff loan you should strike off your list is an unsecured consolidation loan. The fees and interest rates for these kinds of loans are typically outrageous. They'll just stretch out your payments, ultimately costing you much more than if you had paid off your original loans.

#141. If I don't have the money to pay off high-interest loans, what can I do?

Renegotiate your current loan rates. Many banks and credit card issuers would rather lower their interest rates or cut fees than lose you as a customer. If you are paying high rates for credit cards, call each card issuer and threaten to switch over to a lower rate competitor. If they won't budge, make the switch. They may be more willing to negotiate with you if they think you may file for bankruptcy.

#142. I love my car but my car payment is killing me. What should I do?

Minimize what you spend on cars. If you buy a new $25,000 car and drive it off the lot, you instantly lose $5,000 because suddenly your new car is a used car. High car and lease payments are one of the primary reasons why people have no money to save. A car can't be more important than your savings account, can it? Read the section about buying or leasing cars in Chapter 18, where you can learn how to cut back on what you're spending on cars.

#143. What is the primary difference between a fifteen-year and a thirty-year mortgage?

Nothing can save you more money over time than paying off your home mortgage as soon as you can. Typically, people elect to take out thirty-year mortgages because it gives them plenty of time to pay off their home, while offering them lower monthly payments. However, if you can work it into your budget to have a higher monthly mortgage in order to pay off your home faster, it can dramatically improve your financial picture. If you own a home with a thirty-year mortgage, consider what a fifteen-year mortgage can do for you.

If you have a $100,000 thirty-year 7 percent mortgage, your payments are approximately $665 a month. If you finance the same amount for fifteen years, your payments would be $900 a month for a difference of only $235. You would have been able to pay off your home in half the time (fifteen instead of thirty years) and saved yourself $80,000 in interest that you can use for investments. If you can't afford the extra monthly amount required to pay your home off in fifteen years, then consider making extra payments when you can to accelerate the time it takes to pay it off.

#144. What are the advantages of paying off my mortgage?

There are several advantages to paying off your mortgage early. Doing so enables you to acquire something you care about (i.e., your home) that appreciates. It will also substantially reduce the amount of interest you'll pay over time. If you are looking to trade up to a more expensive home, nothing will get you there faster than building equity in your existing house. If you are able to pay off your mortgage before you retire, you will have a big part of your living expenses covered.

#145. Should I consider borrowing money at a lower interest rate to pay off my high interest rate loans?

You may be tempted to implement an instant solution to your immediate debt problem by using a home equity loan or some other type of loan to consolidate your high-interest debts into a single debt. In some situations, consolidation loans make sense if you have honestly addressed and resolved the basic problems that got you into debt in the first place. If you haven't done this, you could be digging yourself into a deeper debt hole. These types of loans usually turn short-term into long-term debt. So, in the long run, you could end up paying more in interest.

#146. **Are there good websites and software application programs that can help me get out of debt?**

Fortunately, there are a number of repayment plan calculators online at websites like Quicken.com. It offers one called the Debt Reduction Planner that is excellent. Similar tools are available in personal finance software applications for about $50 at your local computer supply store.

Chapter 16

GETTING TAX MONEY BACK

People probably experience more anxiety about taxes than they do about any other debt issue. The average American household pays 40 percent of its income in federal, state, and local taxes. Clearly, taxes are one of the biggest hurdles you'll have to overcome to achieve your financial goals. Coupled with inflation, taxes steadily eat away at your wages and investments. Reducing your tax liability can help you pay down some of your debts. In order to do that, you need to have a basic understanding of the tax laws so that you can supplement your financial plan with a well-thought-out tax plan.

#147. Where do I start looking for tax breaks?

Start by knowing what tax bracket you're in. It's a simple question but only 4 percent of people whom we interviewed in 2008 had the right answer. And yet your tax bracket is essential because it tells you how much of any extra earnings such as raises you actually get to keep. Under the U.S. graduated tax system, as income rises so does your tax rate. Currently, the federal tax law has five basic rates: 15 percent, 28 percent, 31 percent, 36 percent, and 39.6 percent. However, there are hidden phase-outs of exemptions and itemized deductions that will, over time, force you into higher tax brackets even if your income doesn't increase.

#148. What is the Alternative Minimum Tax (AMT) all about, and do I need to be concerned about it?

The AMT is a federal tax that affects which tax bracket you fall into, and you need to know about it because it may affect how your taxes are calculated. AMT was created several years ago to boost the taxation of wealthy individuals who use tax shelters to legally avoid taxes. While the intentions of the tax were initially good, the rules haven't kept up with the times. Many middle-income earners now earn enough and spend enough on tax-sheltered items to qualify for AMT.

AMT rules severely restrict the deductions you are allowed to take, including interest deductions on a home. If you borrow money for anything except home improvements, such as to buy a car, you can't deduct the interest.

#149. How can I reduce the amount that gets deducted from my paycheck for taxes?

By the time you get through paying federal, state, and local taxes, you're lucky if you get to keep sixty cents out of every dollar you make. When you are faced with that kind of tax bite, you have to take a proactive position to make sure you're taking full advantage of every legal deduction that you can. Don't overwithhold. One of the biggest mistakes that taxpayers make is allowing the government to withhold more taxes than they owe. If you are getting a large tax refund every year, then you probably fall into this category. You are in effect lending the government interest-free money. Increase your exemptions to lower your payroll tax deductions if, and only if, you have the self-discipline to bank the extra money into a secured savings plan like an IRA. If you don't have the willpower to do that, then keep your deductions high even though you won't be earning any interest.

#150. **Is it really worth it to save every receipt that is tax deductible?**

Treat tax receipts as if they are money, which they are. Would you willingly take a $5 bill out of your wallet, and rip it up into small pieces, even though it's not a lot of money? That is in effect what you are doing if you forget to keep a $20 tax receipt that will be worth a $5 tax refund if you're in the 25 percent tax bracket. Record every tax deduction you come across, even the small ones, in one easy-to-find folder. Even a dollar tax deduction is worth twenty-eight cents (assuming you are in the 28 percent tax bracket) and it only takes a second to deposit the receipt in a conveniently located envelope. Those nickel-and-dime receipts will add up to big bucks at tax return time. You'll also need them if you're ever audited by the IRS. For example, the money you spent for tax return software for your PC, the clothes that you donated to Goodwill, and the money you put in the collection plate at church are all tax deductible.

#151. **How should I store my tax receipts and records?**

Most people dump all of their financial paperwork including tax deduction records into a storage box. At the end of the year, when it comes time to prepare their tax returns, they'll start rummaging through the box in the hope of finding anything that even resembles a tax deduction. There are several problems that arise from this crude procedure. First, it forces you to sort through a whole year's worth of paperwork when you should be concentrating on preparing your tax return. Second, if you are content to dump everything into a box so that you don't have to think about your tax situation until the end of the year, you will miss out on potential deductions.

Here's a better approach for maintaining tax records that is more productive and saves time. At the beginning of each month, write "TAX RECORDS FOR (MONTH/YEAR)" on an envelope. Now, as you go through the month paying tax-related bills, selling stock, or engaging in any tax-related activities (e.g., making charitable donations), insert a record of each activity into the envelope. The form of the record could simply be a receipt for the payment of your property taxes or a handwritten note recording the nonreimbursed mileage driven to a business meeting. When you get to the end of the year, you'll have all of your tax records neatly filed in twelve envelopes.

#152. I'm afraid of the IRS and therefore don't like to prepare my own tax return. Am I overreacting?

Contrary to the popular rumor, the IRS is not a money-hungry monster, ready to pounce on and devour any taxpayer it can catch. The fact of the matter is that a vast majority of taxpayers are left alone. Quite frankly, the agency has bigger fish to go after, like flagrant tax cheaters, as opposed to people who are trying to honestly pay their taxes. Even if you have someone prepare your tax return, you are still responsible for reporting your taxable income and tax deductions. If you make a mathematical error on your tax return, the IRS will correct it, and adjust your return accordingly. If you declare a "questionable" deduction that gets denied by the IRS, your return will be adjusted accordingly. Yes, you will be notified of the correction and its subsequent effect on your return. No, you will not go to jail. What the IRS does not tolerate is tax evasion.

#153. How should I plan for my taxes?

You should plan by starting very early! Most people approach their tax planning strategy backward. They'll sit down for a few hours once a year, sometime between January 1 and April 15, and start sifting through an old shoebox of expense records in the hope of finding some tax deductions. The problem is that by that time, it is too late to take advantage of tax-saving opportunities that have existed all year long. Financially astute people approach the task by always looking ahead, rather than behind, to plan a year-round strategy that will yield the lowest possible tax rate for them on April 15. You won't find them standing in line at the post office just before midnight waiting to mail their returns. If they have a refund due, they've filed their return the same day they received their W2 forms so that they could get their refund early and reinvest the money.

#154. How can I deduct what I spend on home improvements when I sell my home?

If you own a home, keep every receipt of every home improvement you do to increase the value of your property, even if you tell everyone you'll never sell. If you should ever decide to sell, home improvements are tax deductible and can be deducted from capital gains from your home. Home improvements with verifiable receipts also make an excellent selling tool to use on prospective buyers.

#155. What are the advantages and disadvantages of having someone prepare my tax return?

Filling out a tax return is almost as bad as having to go to the dentist—maybe worse. You spend hours digging through and sorting your tax-deductible receipts, tediously filling out a myriad of tax forms, and when you're all done, you're still left with nagging questions: Could I somehow be paying less? Did I take every legitimate deduction that's due me?

A top-notch tax accountant can save you a lot of aggravation and, in many cases, identify deductions that you have overlooked. Let's face it—they know tax laws much better than you do. They're preparing tax returns at least four months out of the year, whereas you spend a couple of days out of the year doing one return. The type of tax accountant you need will depend on the complexity of your return, where you are in your financial plan, and how much you're willing to pay.

#156. Where do I look to find someone to prepare my tax return?

Storefront tax preparers. These are the people who work for companies like H&R Block that maintain storefronts in mini-malls throughout the country. Most of these people are working part-time during the tax season to earn extra money. They have been trained in how to ask you the right questions and fill out tax returns.

Accountants. These are people who have a four-year college degree in accounting or an MBA in accounting. Most of them work as accountants for companies and moonlight out of their home to earn extra money during the tax season. They have an edge over storefront tax preparers since they have accounting degrees and work full-time in the accounting field.

Certified Public Accountants (CPAs). CPAs are considered the tax professionals of the industry. If you have a complex return, need tough questions answered on your current return, require year-round tax and investment planning advice, and help just in case you're audited by the IRS, then you need a CPA. And yes, they are the most expensive as well.

#157. How can I get my money's worth if I elect to have someone prepare my tax return?

Always arrive prepared when you meet with your tax professional. Most of them will be charging you for their services on an hourly basis, so if you waste their time because you're not prepared, you'll pay for it. After your return has been prepared, find out what you can do to reduce your taxes next year. This may require a follow-up visit with your tax preparer after the tax season is over. Or, if you are using a seasonal accountant, ask him for his advice at the same time you're having your return prepared.

Don't assume that tax preparers are experts in everything that's important to you. Do your own research and homework so that you can carry on an informed conversation about key topics. Also, keep your preparer informed about any changes in your family situation that could affect your tax status, like a divorce, new baby, or marriage. If you are considering taking a tax deduction that you think is legally borderline, give them all the facts and ask for their opinion about the risk of an audit. In other words, treat your tax professional as a strategic partner who is interested in helping you achieve your financial goals.

#158. **How can I reduce my property taxes?**

Find out if you qualify for any special property tax exemptions in your state. These exemptions aren't widely publicized by most states. Many states offer exemptions if you're over sixty-five, disabled, a veteran, or in other special group classifications. If you believe your home is assessed too high, document your case before you see the tax assessor. If part of your case is based on the value of comparable properties in your neighborhood, you'll need written verification of three to five comparable homes. Photographs will help strengthen your case, so include those with your documents. Make sure you follow the appeal process of your county's government to the letter. Be polite and control your irritation whenever you talk to county officials. Mad won't cut it if you're trying to solicit their cooperation. If the county appeals board rejects your challenge, you can challenge the board in court at the state level or file your complaint with the state review board. That can be an expensive proposition that will probably require an attorney, so make sure it will be worth your time and money.

Chapter 17

CREATING A
SAVINGS PLAN

This chapter addresses several important savings-related questions such as whether you should save your money or pay off your debts first. A lot of people aren't in the enviable position of having the financial flexibility to do both. The die-hard savers will argue that the more money you have on hand, the better you can survive a financial emergency without running up more debt. The debt-killers will argue that the amount of interest you'll earn in a savings account is usually insignificant in comparison to the interest you're paying on loans. Who's right? Both are. You should begin to develop the discipline it takes to save money (even a small amount) while you're paying off your debts.

#159. Where am I going to find any money to save?

If you are like most people, you spend money on things that you really don't need and the money you make is just enough to cover your expenses. Your first challenge will be to get control over your spending habits and establish a monthly budget for everything you buy. You'll be amazed at how it will help you save on the little things that will add up to big dollars over a relatively short period of time. That is where you'll find the money to save.

Let's take an easy example. Suppose you and your son have season tickets to baseball. If it costs the two of you $15 to eat at the game, you're spending about $200 on food during the season. Suppose you made sandwiches and carried them to the game at an annual cost of $50, thereby saving $150 a year. If you invested the $150 into a mutual fund that averages 10 percent over 20 years, your $150 will be worth $10,000. By making one minor adjustment in your spending and investment priorities, you have made a substantial contribution to your financial future.

#160. I've procrastinated about saving money all of my life. Can you help me get motivated?

Start by tracking your daily expenses on a card that you carry with you, or download a free expense worksheet from American Association of Retired People's website (*www.aarpmagazine.org/money*). Then begin writing down every penny you spend. Look for at least five expenses you can cut that will immediately start saving you money. For example, review your cell phone bill, recreational spending, any unnecessary luxuries, etc. If you have accumulated some major debt, then your first priority should be to pay off the debt and avoid any additional debt.

If you need an extra incentive to see how much the savings of a few dollars a day can transform your financial future, use the calculator at *www.aarpmagazine.org/money*. For instance, let's say you came up with ways to save $10 per day or $70 a week. If you invested that $70 savings every week in an investment that, on average, returns 8 percent annually, you would have saved $2,816 in one year. After five years, you would have $16,470. That number would climb to over $40,000 in ten years.

#161. In general, how much should people save?

It's impossible to give you a set number. But save something every month no matter how much you make or don't make. You must be willing to save every month, even if it means going without something you want. Pay yourself first before you pay any of your bills (revisit Chapter 9). Set savings goals, such as "I want to save 1 percent of my income every month." After you prove to yourself that you did that, slap yourself on the back and double your goal to 2 percent.

#162. Can you give me five painless ways to start saving some money?

Sure. Here are six (you get a bonus!).

1. When you get a raise, deposit the extra amount of money you get directly into your savings account so you won't miss it.
2. Take lunches to work instead of eating out and you will be amazed at how much you'll save.
3. When you get your income tax refund, use it to pay off credit cards and then deposit into your savings account the extra money you'll have because you are not making monthly credit card payments.
4. Deposit any part-time money, overtime pay, and bonus checks into your savings account.
5. Pay cash for everything. It is harder to pay cash than it is to use a credit card, and you'll find yourself passing up impulse purchases.
6. Budget a monthly amount to go into a separate savings account for future purchases, such as a car. This can save you thousands later on for interest on a car loan.

#163. What are passbook savings accounts?

Passbook savings accounts are available in all banks including savings and loan associations and offer the lowest interest rates of all of the savings account vehicles. Use them as a savings vehicle of last resort. They're okay to meet short-term savings needs.

#164. I have heard that Americans on average save less than 1 percent of their income. Why is it so low?

Most of us have been raised in a "spend it while you got it" society. We were taught that debt was good while savings were not good.

The huge buildup of consumer debt has always been a critical component of our national economy. Our entire political system has been geared to endorse our infatuation with debt. Over the past several years, the nation's debt level has climbed from zero dollars to several trillion dollars. The burden of paying that back will fall squarely on your children and grandchildren.

#165. What is a certificate of deposit (CD) and should I consider it as a place to save my money?

A certificate of deposit is money that you give to (deposit with) your bank or credit union to hold on your behalf for a specific period of time at a stipulated interest rate. CDs typically pay a much higher interest rate than passbook accounts. The specified time periods that you are required to hold a CD are typically in 90-day increments. For example, you can invest in a 90-day, 180-day, 360-day, or longer CD. The rate of interest that you earn usually increases with the length of time you elect to hold your CD. At the end of whatever time period you choose, your financial institution "cashes out" your CD and issues you a check that covers your principle and earned interest. If for whatever reason you choose to withdraw your funds from a CD before its maturity date, you will pay a penalty.

CDs are a very safe place to save money that you're holding for the future. Most banks offer them as a convenience at various amounts and maturity dates.

#166. What are money market funds and should I consider them as a place to save my money?

Money market funds (MMFs) are not mutual funds, as the name would imply. They are checking accounts that are loosely tied to the prevailing interest rate and pay interest that is significantly higher than what you get from a passbook savings account. They are offered through the major banks and mutual fund companies and are government insured. They are a great place to deposit your savings, since they offer the convenience of being able to write a check against your account if you need to access the funds. You are required to maintain a minimum balance in most money market accounts, so check with the financial organizations that interest you.

MMF accounts are a special breed of savings account set up by financial institutions. They pay interest rates that are tied to the overall market interest rates. When you deposit money into an MMF account, your money begins to immediately earn interest at the current money market rate. And you can withdraw part or all of your deposit in an account at any time without incurring an early-withdrawal fee. The "no penalty" withdrawal feature gives the edge to MMFs over CDs. Both pay substantially higher interest rates than passbook savings accounts. There is no reason why you would want to keep part or all of your savings in a passbook account over a CD or MMF.

#167. I don't have that much to save. Is the interest rate important, and where should I put my savings?

To answer this question, let's assume you are only able to save $10 a month, or $120 a year, in a 1 percent interest savings passbook account. At the end of the first year, you would have accumulated a whopping $1.20 in interest. The quick and easy answer is that the interest rate is not important, which is the wrong answer. The fact that you managed to save something and earned interest on the money you saved is a significant accomplishment. Had you chosen in this example to save your money in a money market fund, you would have earned five times the interest rate (5 percent) that was earned in a passbook savings account (1 percent). That's important!

#168. What is a good savings strategy to have?

To develop a good savings strategy, you must be financially aware of compound interest and possess a commitment to saving for your future. One of the best ways to make that happen is to have a set dollar amount pulled out of your paycheck and automatically deposited into your savings account. Most payroll departments can help you with the paperwork to set that up. Automatic transfers are also available through the checking account services at most banks.

#169. What is compound interest and how does it affect my savings?

Compounding means that the bank adds the interest you earn to your savings account, and then pays interest on the combined interest and principle. The more often your interest is compounded, the more money you make. Daily or continuous compounding yields the most, which is the method used in most savings accounts. The following table shows how compounding favorably affects your savings:

Compound Interest on a $1,000 Deposit at 6% Interest

Compound Method	1 Year	5 Years	10 Years
Daily	$1,065	$1,350	$1,820
Semiannually	$1,060	$1,340	$1,805
Annually	$1,055	$1,335	$1,790

PART 3

Improving Your Quality of Life

Chapter **18**

ACQUIRING A CAR

Next to your home, a car is one of the most expensive purchases you'll ever make. And, unlike your home, a car typically does not appreciate in value. Before you set out to buy a car, decide what kind of vehicle you will need, what options you must have, and what payments you can afford. How will you use the vehicle? Does the purchase of a new car fit into your budget and financial plan at this time? Should you consider buying a used car? Maybe you should lease one? These are just some of the questions addressed in this chapter.

#170. What questions should I ask before I get a car?

There are several questions to ask yourself and anybody else in your family who will be driving the car:

> What kind of transportation do you need? If you travel a lot, you'll probably want a large interior and a smooth-riding car.

> Will the car be used primarily for commuting to work? Will it be sitting out in the sun all day while you're at work?

> Is fuel economy important to you? How many miles do you drive a year? What will you spend on gasoline per year if you buy a gas-guzzler versus a fuel-efficient car?

If you're thinking about a four-wheel-drive vehicle, will you really use that option? Over 80 percent of four-wheel-drive vehicle owners will never use this expensive option. How much more will four-wheel-drive cost, and is it worth the extra money?

What price are you willing to pay for the car you want and what monthly payments can you afford? How long are you willing to finance the vehicle?

What will it really cost you to run this vehicle annually? Don't just think in terms of gas and oil. Can you afford to maintain the type of vehicle that you want? Check the Consumer Reports guides to find out what the maintenance history is on the type of cars you're considering.

#171. **What does it cost to own a car?**

When a friend asks "How much did your car cost?" you can either tell her what you paid for the thing or tell her what the real cost will be. If you just bought a $25,000 vehicle and are planning on keeping it for five years, your real cost of owning the car will be more than double that amount, or $61,000 to be precise. Using national cost averages collected by the American Automobile Association, here is how that staggering figure was calculated:

The Average Cost of Owning a $25,000 Vehicle over 5 Years

Initial cost of vehicle	$25,000
State sales and other taxes (5%)	$1,250
Acquisition fees (dealer fees, title, etc.)	$500
Auto insurance	$5,000
Total interest on auto loan or lease at 10%	$5,000
State license fees over 5 years	$3,000
Operating and maintenance expense	$6,250
Depreciation	$15,000
Total Operating Cost over 5 Years	$61,000

If you need additional information or help in determining the cost of owning a car, buy a copy of *The Complete Car Cost Guide* that is published by Intellichoice. Edmunds car-buying guides are available on the web (*www.edmunds.com*). Edmunds has long been considered one of the best resources for its outstanding reviews of new and used vehicles.

#172. **How can I get the best car loan possible?**

Don't finance a car for longer than you expect to keep it. If you plan to keep it for four years, take out a four-year loan—or, better yet, take out a three-year loan. You'll save on interest payments and won't be "upside down" in the car, the industry's term for owing more on the car than it's worth if and when you trade it in. Watch out for up-front fees that some lenders add to raise the cost of their loans.

> **Credit union loans.** If you belong to a credit union, these loans are sometimes hard to beat. The amount of money that you have for the down payment can dramatically affect the interest rate that you'll pay. You'll pay a premium if you have less than 10 percent down and many lenders won't even talk to you unless you have at least that.

> **Dealer financing.** The best time to finance a new car is when dealers are advertising finance rates that are significantly below the market rates. Their very best rates usually carry a short repayment term like two years, so you'll need a good payment-free trade or lots of money for the down payment.

> **Bank financing.** You won't get the title to the car until the loan is paid off, and you will be required to carry collision and comprehensive insurance with perhaps lower deductibles than what you normally carry. The best type of a bank loan to get is a simple interest loan with no prepayment penalties.

#173. I've decided to get rid of my car. What options and issues should I consider?

If you've decided to get rid of your current vehicle, one of the nagging questions in your mind is how you will dispose of Old Faithful. You can sell it to a private party or dealer, trade it in for another car, or donate it to a charity and take the tax deduction. What's your asking price and the lowest offer you'll accept? If you want a premium price, then why does it deserve that higher price? Low mileage definitely deserves a higher price. Add at least 10 percent to 15 percent to your price so that you have room to negotiate. The Kelley Blue Book provides pricing information on new and used vehicles. It's available in most major bookstores, or you can visit their web site at *www.kbb.com*.

If you're thinking about trading it in to a dealer for another car, you'll be lucky to get Kelley's Blue Book wholesale price for it. Dealers can buy cars just like yours at wholesale auctions any time they want, so don't expect them to give you a premium for your "one-of-a-kind" jewel. You are usually better off selling it on your own rather than trading it in. Whichever way you decide to go, wash and polish everything including the tires. Nothing will turn off a buyer faster than a car that looks like the inside of a garbage can, so clean everything, including the interior.

#174. What are the advantages of buying a used vehicle?

Although owning a new car is nice, there are many reasons to buy a good used car including the fact that they're cheaper. Registration, license fees, and insurance premiums are usually much lower for used cars. When you buy used, you don't have to pay the destination charges, dealer preparation fees, and shipping charges that go along with buying a new car. According to Consumer Reports, a new car depreciates 20 percent to 30 percent the moment you drive it off the lot. You don't have that problem when you buy used. A well-built and -maintained car will continue to run past 150,000 miles before it needs major engine work. A rebuilt engine costs a lot less than a new vehicle. Usedcars.com provides information about buying used cars. Other sites include *www.cars.com* and *www.auto trader.com*. These site feature classified ads by Zip Code and includes links to other websites including manufacturers, dealers, auto parts stores, and accessories. As well, check out Auto Trader Online (*www.traderonline.com*), Kelley Blue Book's Classifieds (*www.kbb .com*), Online Auto (*www.onlineauto.com*), or Auto Web Interactive (*www.autoweb.com*).

#175. **Should I consider leasing a car?**

When you lease, you are actually renting a car for a specified period of time. Because you don't own it, you are obligated under a lease contract to maintain the vehicle and drive it a limited number of miles per year. If you try to get out of a lease before it expires, you will be required to pay significant penalties. Lease payments are not based on the total value of the car, but rather on the depreciation during the time you lease the vehicle. That's why your monthly payments are typically lower than what they would be if you financed the car for the same period as a purchase. This is one of the reasons why the popularity of leases has increased to about one-third of all new car transactions. That doesn't necessarily mean that leasing makes sense for you. Take a moment and answer the following questions to determine if leasing is right for you:

1. Do you typically trade in a new car every four years or less?
2. Do you, on average, drive less than 15,000 miles a year?
3. Do you keep your vehicle in good condition and follow routine maintenance schedules?
4. Are you self-employed and can you deduct all or part of the lease from your tax return?
5. Do you want a new car every few years for whatever reason?

If you answered yes to three or more of those questions, then you should seriously consider leasing.

#176. I'm considering buying a new car. How are they priced?

If you're thinking about buying a new car, brace yourself for one of the most challenging consumer experiences you will ever have. The new car purchasing process puts you on a playing field pitted against well-trained and intelligent salespeople.

Before you go car shopping, stop by your local library and check out the recent copy of Consumer Reports' *New Car Buying Guide*, which features information on the performance and maintenance records of the major models. It's important to know how new cars are priced when you start shopping so that you can negotiate the best deal. Here's how new cars are priced:

Manufacturers suggested retail price (MSRP). The MSRP is the suggested price that is provided by auto manufacturers for cars. It's their way of assuring that all of their dealers are using standard pricing.

Sticker Price. The sticker price is the total amount that appears in the car's window. Federal law requires all new car dealers to post the base price of the car along with the cost of the options that are installed on the car.

Factory invoice price. The factory invoice price never appears on the car window. It is usually hidden in the sales manager's file drawer. In theory, the invoice price is what the dealer paid the manufacturer for the car.

Visit *www.autosite.com* if you want to find dealer invoice prices or find out about the maintenance records on cars that interest you. For a comprehensive car-buying guide, go to *www.edmunds.com*.

#177. How do I find an honest and reasonable automotive repair facility?

Finding a good automotive repair facility can be challenging and frustrating at the same time, particularly if you've just run into problems with your car. Here are repair shop options for you to consider:

Dealerships. Most car buyers tend to use the dealership's service department when their car is still under warranty. The dealers like that because they want you to return for another new car when you're ready, and, of course, they also want your very profitable service business. They are more expensive but guarantee their work.

National chains. National chains like Midas and Firestone are generally less expensive than dealerships. Many are franchise operations so you could be dealing with a national chain that's owned locally. Most of them offer a wide range of repair services and guarantee their work.

Independent shops. A good independent shop can be your best option. You can usually communicate directly with the owner or head technician who, over time, gets to know your car. If you are a AAA member, the association can provide you with a list of approved facilities as well a rough estimate of costs (i.e., high, medium, or low).

Inner Auto Parts offers an online service (*www.innerauto.com*) where you can find lots of information like how to choose a mechanic and how to maintain your transmission and engine. Theautoshop.com also offers helpful advice and information. Consumer Reports Online (*www.consumerreports.com*) offers helpful information on warranties as well as the maintenance and service statistics for new and used cars.

#178. How can I reduce the cost of my car insurance?

Heightened competition among auto insurers, coupled with safer driving and fewer claims, has kept auto insurance rates from going through the roof. However, the fact remains that your auto insurance probably is the highest monthly premium you're paying on any of your insurance policies. Here are some ways to bring down your cost:

Don't overinsure. Most states require a minimum amount of liability insurance, but the other types of coverage are usually optional. You may not need collision and comprehensive coverage on an older car if its value is less than ten times the annual premium.

Consider raising your deductible for comprehensive and collision. Going from a $250 deductible to $500 or even $1,000 can reduce your insurance cost by 15 percent to 20 percent annually.

Take advantage of discounts if you drive less than the average number of miles per year, install an alarm system, get married, or are over a certain age.

There are a number of websites on the Internet to help you compare rates. Progressive Insurance's site (*www.progressive.com*) will offer you a company quote and up to three quotes from major insurers. Quicken at *quicken.intuit.com* offers online quotes plus e-mailed bids from insurers.

Chapter 19

MAKING MORE MONEY

Yes, you are working hard to make ends meet, but sometimes the only way to dig out from under debt is to earn some extra money. According to the Bureau of Labor Statistics, four out of ten Americans are working a second job. Why? Because they need the money to meet their regular living expenses. Moonlighting—holding a second job in addition to a regular one—can take many different forms.

#179. If I decide to moonlight, do I need to let my employer know what I'm doing?

Most companies don't have written policies on moonlighting. However, it goes without saying that most do not encourage their employees to moonlight. They are concerned that the extra hours one of their employees spends moonlighting will distract him from his regular job. If you decide to moonlight, you are probably better off not disclosing your intent to moonlight in the interest of protecting your regular job. Be sure to check your company's employee handbook if one is available.

#180. How do I start looking for a second job?

Looking for a part-time job is much like the steps you went through to find your full-time job. Scan the classified job ads and surf the ɔn the Internet to find leads. Be sure to check out the services as well. When the regular job market is weak, the temp̲ᵣ   ᵧ job market can compensate for the difference. Temporary services cut across all occupations and time slots around the clock.

#181. Should I consider quitting my current job and getting one that pays more?

If you decide to take that action, make sure you have a minimum salary figure and fringe benefits in mind that you would accept. You may be able to get the extra money you need from your current job. If it has been a while since you've received a raise, ask for one. If for whatever reason you don't get it, ask your supervisor or manager what you need to do to get a raise. If you get nondescript and meaningless answers, then maybe it is time to review all of your options.

#182. I have always dreamed of starting a home-based business. How can I find out more about them?

There's a catalog called the *Small Business Catalog* that you can order free by calling 800-947-7724. Home business guides are featured in the catalog for about $40 per guide, which is a bargain compared to what you'll spend when you actually move into the start-up process. Each guide shows you how to start up a specific home business. You can also order supplemental videos for any of the businesses featured. The catalog offers an easy and inexpensive way to review what the editors consider are the best weekend or full-time home business opportunities. The *Adams Businesses You Can Start Almanac, Second Edition* published by the editors of Adams Media features 500 start-up businesses complete with cost requirements, potential earnings, and the equipment you'll need to get started.

#183. How can I make sure that if I start a home business, it will have a good chance of taking off?

Create a dynamic business plan in writing so that you can focus on what you are doing and give your business direction. At a minimum, your business plan should identify your target market with a clear definition of the types of customers who will most likely buy your products or services, where they live, and how you will sell to them. Your plan should also include a twelve-month and three-year cash flow projection that shows all of the sources and dollar amounts for monthly income, expenses, and estimated profits or losses.

The following checklist will also help make sure your home business succeeds:

1. Get a good accountant. An accountant can show you how to save thousands of dollars on legitimate tax deductions if you keep good records. Keep your tax records straight by keeping receipts for all legitimate business expenses.

2. Open a separate business bank account. It is important from a tax standpoint that you keep business-related expenses and income separate from your personal expenses. Get a business license from your city and state, which will entitle you to buy products at wholesale from a number of wholesale outlets in your area.

3. Always have a separate telephone number for your home business. You won't impress any customers who call and get your four-year-old on the phone while they are trying to order something.

4. You must be able to accept payments from Visa and Mastercard. Yes, there is a service fee that you'll have to pay, but you don't want to turn down a sale because you can't accept a customer's card.

Chapter **20**

BUYING A HOME

Buying a home is an investment subject that deserves special consideration because it can work for you during all the ups and downs of the economic cycle. During inflationary periods, home values typically go up at rates that beat the inflation. And when a recession hits, you still benefit from one of the best tax shelters there is. During much of the 1990s, real estate was almost a "can't lose" investment. Cooling markets in many areas of the country in 2008 combined with more stringent home mortgage qualification standards have made home investments somewhat less alluring, at least in the short term. Yet a home remains a worthwhile component in a well-balanced financial plan and, if chosen properly, will reward you with a consistent rate of return that will do quite well during inflationary periods.

#184. Why is a home a smart investment?

The basic home is still one of the best real estate investments you can make. It's also a great tax shelter, and if you work it right, a home that is paid for when you retire can become the anchor of your retirement plan. Some would argue that the appreciation of private homes has lagged behind Standard & Poor's stock market average over the past ten years. However, their numbers can be deceiving. Let's suppose you bought a $100,000 home and invested

$100,000 into the stock exchange ten years ago. Over that period of time, the average annual appreciation of your home would have been 6 percent, while you would have enjoyed a 13 percent average annual appreciation on your stocks.

This scenario should also ask the question "Why would you have wanted to invest in a home instead of the stock market ten years ago?" When you bought the house in this scenario, let's assume that you were able to negotiate a $100,000 mortgage with a 20 percent ($20,000) down payment. This was not the case when you bought $100,000 in stock. You had to come up with $100,000 out of your personal account to make the trade because it's illegal to borrow money to buy stocks.

Here's the revised bottom line at the end of ten years. Your house would have been worth approximately $185,000, or $85,000 more than you paid for it, based on an initial investment of $20,000. Your stock would have more than doubled over the same period to approximately $210,000, or $110,000 more on your initial investment of $100,000. Yes, you doubled your money in the stock market, but you made over four times the $20,000 you initially invested in your home ($85,000/$20,000 = 4.25).

#185. **What can I afford and what type of home should I buy?**

Keep in mind that it is really not the price of the home that you can afford but rather the mortgage you can afford. As a general rule, your mortgage payment including property taxes and insurance should not exceed 25 percent of your disposable income. The type of home you should buy is of course a matter of personal preference. Newer or new homes can offer you incentives to lower mortgage costs and down payments. New homes are covered under warranty for a period of time, which allows you to not spend money on remodeling and maintenance. If you're not concerned about the price of gasoline, you may be able to afford more house if you are willing to drive farther to commute to work.

#186. **Where can I find bargains on homes?**

Microsoft's MSN Real Estate website (*www.realestate.msn.com*) covers every step of the buying process from researching neighborhoods to applying for a mortgage. The site also allows you to visit over 500,000 listings throughout the country. Consider buying a fixer-upper if you are handy with tools and paintbrushes. A structurally sound house that is priced 20 percent to 30 percent below market because it needs some "tender loving care" could be a good investment. To make sure we are all on the same page, tender loving care means a home needs cosmetic care and not expensive structural repairs like replacing a cracked slab.

Look for distress situations where a seller has to put a house on the market for a quick sale because of a job transfer, a divorce settlement, or to settle an estate. Never be afraid to submit an offer that is substantially less than the asking price. If your realtor balks, get another one. If you can, buy the cheapest house in the neighborhood. The higher-priced homes will tend to pull the value of yours up as they appreciate. If you are at the higher-price end of the neighborhood, you'll restrict your buying opportunities when you sell. Some people like to buy down rather than buy up!

Also, you may want to consider buying a home that is in foreclosure where the owners have turned their property over to the lender. Foreclosures have reached their highest level in years and lenders are often anxious to resell their foreclosures to qualified buyers at discount rates.

#187. **What are the costs of owning a home versus renting one?**

There are extra expenses to consider when figuring your budget for a home purchase versus renting. You will pay property taxes, which could vary from 1 percent to 3 percent of your home's value. You will need to protect your investment with homeowners insurance, which can add $25 a month per $100,000 of valuation. If you are a first-time home buyer and are unable to come up with a 20 percent down payment, which most financial institutions require since our mortgage meltdown in 2006–2007, you may have to pay private mortgage insurance on the part of the loan that covers the 20 percent down payment. This is to protect the financial institution from risks and can cost as much as $43 per $100,000 of your mortgage. Also, $150 a month for repairs and maintenance costs needs to be factored in. Here is an example of a comparison of renting a $900-a-month apartment versus owning a $150,000 home:

The Added Cost of Owning a Home

Monthly Expenses	Cost of Homeowner Big-Ticket Items	Monthly Expenses	Cost of Homeowner Big-Ticket Items
Mortgage Loan	$1,000	Water Softener	$1,100
Property Tax	$155	Insect Control	$400
Home Insurance	$40	Snow Blower	$2,000
Maintenance	$65	Lawn Mower	$200
Home Repairs	$150	Sprinkler System	$1,500
TOTAL	$1,410	TOTAL	$5,200

Instead of $1,000 in rent, your investment becomes $1,410! There will be an additional cost you will have as a homeowner as well. To this figure, add utilities (heat, air conditioning, water, sewer, garbage pickup, etc.). You will also need to landscape and maintain the outside lawn and garden, driveways, and sidewalks in summer and winter. These additional costs can add another 30 percent to 40 percent to your basic mortgage costs.

#188. Can I afford to purchase a home?

Put yourself through a trial play-house test by renting for six, nine, or twelve months. If you pay $1,000 a month in rent, put aside in a separate savings account an additional $400 (40 percent) to cover the extra expenses that were covered in the previous question. If you are unable to save that extra amount after putting the maximum amount of dollars away to match your employer-sponsored 401(k) plan, then you are not ready to purchase a home. Remember, don't run up credit cards or take out a new auto loan while you are saving the down payment (20 percent) for your home. Then, if you can put away the extra money without running out of cash before the end of the month, you will be ready to buy a home.

#189. What should I look for before I buy a home?

Thoroughly inspect any home you're thinking about buying. Read books that show you how to conduct your own home inspection and consult with knowledgeable friends who can help you determine if the house is in good shape. If it's an older home, hire a professional home inspector to conduct a survey for you. Let your fingers do the walking through the Yellow Pages to find one. Many states require home inspectors to be licensed. Ask the seller to include a home warranty in the selling price when you submit an offer. A typical warranty covers major home systems like plumbing, heating, and electrical equipment. Home warranties also protect the seller from possible legal action resulting from their failure to disclose known defects in the house before it was sold. Lower your consumer debt so that you'll have a better chance to qualify for a higher loan. Even if your mortgage rate and payments are higher than what you wanted, you can always refinance or prepay the loan down.

#190. Should I buy a condominium instead of a house?

If routine home maintenance, like mowing the yard, is not something that you want to do, you may want to consider buying a condominium. Condominiums are homes that are attached to one another thereby sharing common walls. You own a unit and share common grounds such as recreational areas with the other condominium owners through what is called a homeowners' association. One of the major advantages condominiums have over freestanding houses is that they generally cost less to buy and require less upkeep. Each owner pays a monthly maintenance fee to the homeowners' association to maintain the exterior walls of each condominium and to provide landscaping services. You do not own the land under the unit—that's owned by the association.

Single-family homes generally have a greater potential for capital appreciation than condominiums if they're located in an area where property values have consistently risen over the past several years. Quite often, small investments in cosmetics such as paint and landscaping can substantially improve their selling price. They offer more privacy than what you will find in a condominium since you are not sharing a common wall with your neighbor. However, since you are responsible for all maintenance work, you can expect to spend more to maintain a home than you would a condominium. You own the land under and around your home.

#191. If I decide to move, should I rent or buy a home?

The answer to that depends on your personal situation, but here are some things to think about. To help you get started, go to *www. wellsfargo.com/challenge*. Wells Fargo has an extensive site about home buying, including workshops and seminars for the prospective home buyer. If you decide to rent, understand that you are paying someone else's mortgage and helping them experience the appreciation and tax advantages of owning property. However, renting is sometimes advantageous when you move to a new area and are not sure where you want to live, or you decide to build a house and need temporary shelter during the process. Don't rule out renting because it really depends on your situation and needs. Weigh the pros and cons of owning versus renting to determine which solution works best for you.

#192. How can I assess a good purchase price on a home?

Before you go out with a realtor to shop for a home, you need to do some preliminary homework on pricing. The best way to do this is to look at open houses in the area you are interested in. Keep track of what real estate is doing in your area of interest while you are renting and saving for your down payment. Your local paper should have, by Zip Codes, the recent average sales prices of homes and condos in your target area. You can start your own housing spreadsheet to assess what the values are so that when you are ready to buy, you do not overpay. How long are homes sitting on the market in your target area? Are they selling above or below the listing prices? If homes are selling within ninety days and are at or close to full list price, you are at a disadvantage as a buyer because it is a "sellers' market." However, if homes are lingering for months on the market and selling way below their asking price, congratulations—you are in a "buyers' market" and that is to your advantage.

#193.   **What do I need to know about mortgages?**

Most homes are financed with a loan secured by a deed of trust, commonly referred to as a mortgage. Mortgages are available from many sources, including commercial banks, savings and loan associations, credit unions, insurance companies, and mortgage companies. Most lenders offer fully amortized loans in which you repay the principle (borrowed amount) and the interest over a specified period of time. At first, most of your payment goes toward the interest. As you continue to make payments over time, an increasing part of your payment goes to pay off the principle and a decreasing part goes to interest. The interest on most loans is classified as either fixed-rate or variable-rate.

In fixed-rate loans, the interest rate and your monthly payments remain the same over the term of the loan, which is usually fifteen or thirty years. Variable-rate loans offer an interest rate that fluctuates with the market interest rate. They are usually indexed to the "prime rate" plus points. The prime rate is the preferred interest rate that is offered by lending institutions to their best corporate customers. The prime rate will fluctuate up or down at any one point in time with changes in the economy. A point is equivalent to one interest point, so if a bank offers you a variable-rate mortgage at prime plus two points, and prime is at 6 percent, you'll pay 8 percent interest.

#194. **How does my FICO score affect my mortgage rate?**

Your FICO score will be a major factor in determining the interest rate you'll pay for a home mortgage. In general, the lower your score, the higher the interest rate you'll be charged. The following table will give you an idea of higher interest rates and how it will affect your mortgage.

Monthly Mortgage Costs

Interest Rate	$100,000	$200,000	$300,000
4%	$477	$955	$1,432
5%	$537	$1,074	$1,610
6%	$600	$1,200	$1,800
7%	$665	$1,330	$1,995
8%	$734	$1,467	$2,310

#195. **Can I shop for a mortgage on the Internet?**

An increasing number of savvy home buyers are seeking home loans on the Internet. Over a billion dollars in home loans are already flowing through Internet channels. There are several home mortgage sites on the Internet that offer different levels of service. Here are a few of the better sites to check:

E-Loan at *www.eloan.com*. E-Loan offers mortgages from sixty lenders to home buyers in thirty-nine states. They will handle the entire transaction online and with Federal Express for document delivery.

HomeShark at *www.homeshark.com*. HomeShark offers a service that is similar to E-Loan. They represent several lenders that operate out of forty-six states. You can also search their home sellers' database of 1 million homes nationwide.

QuickenMortgage at *www.quickenmortgage.com*. Intuit offers a service that lets you compare rates and terms with eleven national lenders. If you select one of the lenders, you work with that lender to close the loan.

MSN Real Estate at *www.realestate.msn.com*. This is Microsoft's new service, which is similar to Intuit's service. Its aim is to become an overall home-buying service.

Chapter 21

PROTECTING YOURSELF WITH INSURANCE

Even though you may be up to your neck in debt and insurance is the last thing on your "must have" list, you still need to consider all of your insurance options.

If you don't have any insurance or a sufficient amount of the right insurance, everything you own can be in jeopardy. A single sickness or accident could wipe you out. If you think it could never happen to you, think again!

Your insurance plan should be an important part of your overall financial plan. It should cover your financial needs in the event that a disaster adversely affects you financially. If you're married and living off two incomes, you and your spouse need to address the financial ramifications of one of you dying prematurely. Could the surviving spouse sustain his or her lifestyle on a single income? If children are involved, the scenario needs to be expanded to cover their financial needs if one or both of you were to die before they reach adulthood.

#196. **What's the difference between term and whole life insurance, and do I even need life insurance when I'm trying to get out of debt?**

You don't need any life insurance if no one whom you care about will suffer from the financial consequences of your untimely death. If this statement applies to you, then skip the questions on life insurance.

Like auto insurance or homeowners insurance, term insurance buys you pure protection at lower cost than whole life insurance. The premiums are usually paid annually at a set term and increase as you age. Its sole function is to provide financial support to your family or people you care about if you die. On the surface, term insurance would seem to be preferable to whole life since it is considerably cheaper.

Term policies end in a specified number of years, such as ten or twenty. If you still need insurance coverage when your term policy runs out, you can always renew it if you're in good health. If you develop health problems like high blood pressure, you may be uninsurable, which is a major disadvantage of term insurance. Term insurance is great if you need a lot of cheap life insurance coverage over a specified number of years while you simultaneously replace the protection it provides by building your investment portfolio. Whole life insurance remains in effect for the rest of your life, regardless of your physical condition.

#197. **How much life insurance do I really need?**

If you are young, single, and have no dependents, you probably don't need any life insurance. If you're married and have children, one approach would be to multiply the combined incomes of you and your spouse by the number of years your children will be dependents to get a ballpark minimum coverage figure. For example, let's assume that you and your spouse have a combined annual income of $75,000. You have two children, ages eight and ten, who you have decided will remain dependents until they reach the age of eighteen. The amount of life insurance coverage could be calculated as follows:

$$
\begin{aligned}
\text{Coverage} \quad &= (\text{Combined Incomes}) \times (\text{Dependent Years} \\
&\qquad \text{Remaining} \,/\, \text{Number of Dependents}) \\
&= (\$75,000) \times (10 + 8) \,/\, 2 \\
&= \$75,000 \times 9 \text{ years} \\
&= \$675,000
\end{aligned}
$$

Each spouse would need to purchase a life insurance policy equal to one half of the total amount needed, or \$337,500, to be able to cover the lost income if one of them were to die. In this example, it was arbitrarily assumed that each spouse earns the same amount of money, or \$37,500 a year, to simplify the illustration.

#198. Is there any way to save on life insurance premiums?

When you shop for life insurance, contact at least two companies that you can negotiate with at the same time. All of them have different life products to offer at widely varying fees. You can check their ability to pay in the event of a death by the company's rating, which is AAA for the highest rating, BBB for the next best, and so on. You can find insurance company ratings on the web at *www .insure.com.*

Select an insurance agent that you are comfortable with and who is willing to present the pros and cons of several different life insurance policies.

Establish a baseline of what you need. In the interest of keeping it simple, get a price for a plain-vanilla term life policy in the amount that you need. It is the cheapest form of life insurance offered. You buy a specified amount of coverage (e.g., \$100,000) for a term of years (e.g., twenty years). At the end of the term, the policy expires. It is as simple as that. All insurance companies would prefer to sell you a whole life policy, or a derivative thereof, rather than a cheap term policy because there is more money in it for them. Whole life policies pay off when you die and typically build up a cash value over time.

As you would expect, they cost a lot more than a term policy. Again, compare their cost and added features to what you would pay for a term policy so that you can make an intelligent decision as to what's best for you. If you are heavily in debt, a plain term policy may be all that you can afford at this time.

#199. What do the many categories of auto insurance cover and which ones do I need?

The following list covers a description of auto insurance options along with a brief explanation of what's important:

> **Bodily injury liability.** Liability coverage protects you financially if your car injures or kills someone. Because you could be liable for a large sum, you should obtain as much of this coverage as you can afford. Because of your debt situation, you may have to settle for the minimum liability amount that is required by your state.

> **Property damage liability.** If you are at fault, property damage pays for the damage that your car causes to another person's car, but it also covers any damage your car might do to other property, such as a trailer or a home. Because of your debt situation, you may have to settle for the minimum liability amount that is required by your state.

> **Medical payments.** This pays for medical bills from injuries suffered in an accident. It's a relatively inexpensive form of medical insurance and pays the medical bills for anybody injured in your car regardless of who was at fault.

> **Collision and comprehensive coverage.** Collision coverage pays for damage to your vehicle, no matter who is at fault. Premiums vary with the value of a vehicle and the amount of the deductible. If you are driving an older car, it may not pay to buy collision coverage, unless it would cost you a lot more to replace what you have currently. Comprehensive coverage picks up where collision leaves off. It insures your vehicle

against theft, damage from falling objects, earthquakes, floods, or collisions with animals.

Uninsured and underinsured motorist coverage. This covers you if you're involved in an accident with an uninsured driver or a driver who is underinsured.

#200. What is disability insurance and do I need it?

Do you need it? Yes, if you are working in a high personal-risk job like construction. Disability insurance pays you a monthly income if you are not able to work because of an illness or an accident. You insure yourself for a specified sum of money, such as $5,000 a month or whatever you need to get by. You may already have disability insurance, so check with your human resources department to find out if you're covered. You can buy individual coverage that can be standalone coverage or a supplement to coverage you already have. Most major insurance companies offer some form of disability insurance. Many professional and trade associations offer different forms of inexpensive disability insurance. If you don't have disability insurance, see if it is available through an organization that you belong to. Because of your debt situation, you may not be able to afford disability insurance at this time.

#201. Everybody needs health insurance but I can't afford it. What can I do?

Explore as many options as you can, and find something that you can afford. You need a health plan that will insure your continued good health. Without health insurance, it will be difficult for you to find a doctor, and you could even be turned away from a hospital emergency room unless it is a life-or-death situation. Health insurance premiums have risen significantly in the past four years alone with no end in sight.

Health maintenance organization (HMO) plans are "managed care" plans in which you are limited as to the doctors you can go to, since the doctors must be in the plan. You may need to pay to see a provider doctor in order to get a script or a referral to a doctor outside of the HMO plan. A preferred provider organization (PPO) plan gives you more flexibility in choosing your doctor and getting tests approved for payment. As a general rule, the more flexibility you have in choosing your doctors, the greater the cost of the plan.

If you have health insurance where you work and you leave your employer, check into the availability of COBRA coverage. COBRA (Consolidated Omnibus Budget Reconciliation Act) was an act passed by Congress in 1986 that allows former employees of a company to keep their company health plan for at least eighteen to thirty-six months after leaving the company. Blue Cross and Blue Shield are mandated to insure all people without regard to most of the criteria commercial insurers normally use. Blue Cross is readily available if you are willing to pay their high premiums. Many trade and professional associations now offer medical insurance policies for their members.

#202. **What is the best way to shop for affordable health care insurance?**

First, eliminate insurers that for any reason make you feel uncomfortable, such as those who refuse to insure you for preexisting conditions. Second, consult a knowledgeable associate and use her judgment to help narrow the field. Find out if health insurance is available from any organizations to which you belong. Many religious, fraternal, and professional organizations provide health insurance for their members at competitive rates.

If you have health insurance at work and are looking for ways to reduce the cost, ask your benefits person if there is a less expensive plan you could switch to. If you are paying for your own insurance, go to *www.ehealthinsurance.com* to see if there is a less expensive plan to switch to. If you join an HMO, make sure you know their rules and whom to call if there is ever a question. If you don't follow their rules, they may not pay your medical bills.

With a few smart moves, you can cut your prescription drug bills by 50 percent or more. If your doctor prescribes a brand-name drug, always ask if there is a generic equivalent. Partnership for

Prescription Assistance (*www.pparx.com*; 888-477-2669) provides a centralized data bank that makes it easy to learn about over 250 public and private discount drug programs.

#203. I'm paying a fortune for homeowners insurance. Is there any way I can reduce my premium?

Most homes are insured with a homeowners policy that combines property insurance and personal liability insurance into a single policy. The property portion of the insurance covers your home, its furnishings, and your personal belongings. The personal liability part covers individuals or members of a household against claims from third parties who may have sustained an injury while they were on your property. If your home was destroyed by a fire, you would have to spend a considerable amount of money to replace not only your home but your furnishings as well. One of the best opportunities you have to save money on your homeowners policy without taking on significant additional risk is in the personal property part of your policy, which carries a deductible. The deductible could range anywhere from $0 to $250, $500, $1,000, or more. The higher the deductible, the less you'll pay.

Don't overinsure. If your house is worth $100,000 and you insure it for $200,000 and it gets destroyed by fire, the most you'll get is $100,000. That's the way the insurance system works. Don't underinsure for the same reason. If your house is worth $200,000 and you insure it for $100,000, you'll only get $100,000. Install deadbolts, fire detectors, a fire extinguisher, and a burglar alarm (even a cheap one), and you'll get a discount on your insurance. Ask about "replacement value" insurance that does not depreciate your assets regardless of age.

#204. My home is in what they call a low to medium area for floods. Do I need flood insurance?

Yes. Approximately 25 percent of the flood insurance claims come from the flood risk areas (e.g., the Midwest). If you are living in a floodplain area, you need flood insurance. Premiums for flood insurance are expensive, but if you have watched a news broadcast showing homes caught in a major flood, you should have an appreciation for the fact that your home can be completely destroyed by a flood. The Federal Emergency Management Agency (FEMA) offers a National Flood Insurance Program (NFIP) that is available in communities that adopt and enforce regulations to reduce flood losses.

For more information about NFIP, call their office at 888-379-9531 or visit their website at *www.fema.gov*. They can tell you if your area is covered and what its flood risks are. FEMA's guidelines for assessment of risk are based on an anticipated 100-year flood event. If you live near a major river that has a levee, you would be well advised to include flood insurance in your homeowners policy. If the levee gives out before a 100-year flood, you will have protected all of your home and its furnishings. Flooding is happening more frequently, particularly in the Midwest, as we saw in 2008.

#205. I've heard that credit insurance is a waste of money. Is it?

Credit insurance guarantees a lender's loan in the event of your demise, and the companies that sell credit insurance policies make a lot of money off them. It is one of the most expensive decreasing term insurance policies that you can buy. In most cases, you are not the beneficiary of the policy. The lender is the beneficiary of a policy that you pay for. They are not a good deal.

#206. Does it make any sense to get dental insurance?

It depends. Dental insurance comes packaged in three general types of policies:

1. A basic policy will cover routine examinations and cleaning.
2. A maintenance policy extends the basic policy to cover some dental work like fillings.
3. A comprehensive policy covers major dental work that is specifically identified in the wording of the policy.

As you increase the options that a dental policy offers, your premiums increase accordingly. Now, do you need dental insurance? If your teeth are in good condition, then you probably do not need it. If they are not in good condition, then you may need dental insurance. One of the best ways to find out is to get a comprehensive dental exam complete with a list of what dental work needs to be done and the cost to restore to "good" the condition of your teeth. Once you know this, you are in a position to shop for a dental policy that meets your needs.

#207. How are insurance deductibles established and how can I use them to my advantage?

An insurance deductible is what you will pay, out of your pocket, before you collect the balance due to you by your insurance provider. For example, if you have a $100 deductible on your health care plan, then you will be responsible for paying the first $100 before your insurance will begin to pay for the rest of your care. You can use deductibles to your advantage because the higher the deductible, the less the insurance plan will cost you. Also, you can often deduct these from your taxes. This can give you some breathing room when it comes to health care costs. For example, if you get a minimal deductible, such as $100, then you will pay more each month than a plan with, say, a $1,000 deductible.

#208. Can I get discounts for using the same insurance provider for multiple policies?

Yes. You can usually get a discount on the cost of insurance when you buy all of your insurance from one company. Purchasing your home, car, and health insurance from one provider can save you hundreds of dollars. It is worth getting several quotes from reputable companies and inquiring about combining all of your insurance under their umbrella. Once you have their quote, compare the quotes and coverage with other reputable companies to find the best rates.

Chapter **22**

THINKING ABOUT RETIRING

Why should you even be thinking about retirement when you're surrounded by debt? Unfortunately, 60 percent of Americans are heavily in debt when they retire. They are subsequently forced to substantially cut back on their standard of living when they retire and many have to work part-time just to make ends meet. The rest have made a successful transition into retirement because they were debt free. Those who managed and invested their money wisely were able to leave the corporate world and begin enjoying the fruits of their labor.

Whenever you plan to retire, you are bound to encounter some sleepless nights wondering whether or not you'll have enough money to live on for the rest of your life. Will you be able to get your debts under control and invest your money wisely so that you can retire? There are several questions that you need to think about before you retire that will be covered in this chapter.

#209. Am I ready to retire and can I afford it?

To help you answer the question, following is a questionnaire that looks at some of the questions you may face. Answer yes or no to each question. "Maybe" answers are not allowed.

134

1. Have you developed a retirement plan that clearly identifies what you want to accomplish before and after you retire?
2. Do you know how much money you'll need to support a retirement lifestyle that's acceptable to you?
3. Have you identified the exact sources of income that you expect to receive after you retire?
4. Do you have any dependents that you must take care of after you retire?
5. If yes, do you have a plan in place for how you'll handle this?
6. If you retire before you are eligible for Medicare (age sixty-five), will you have medical insurance that covers you?

If this retirement questionnaire created more questions in your mind than answers, you may want to concentrate your efforts on the questions in the book that address your specific concerns.

#210. What are the greatest fears people have when they retire?

There's no question that the biggest fear for people when it comes to retirement is financial. Will they have enough money to support themselves and their dependents throughout their retirement years? According to *Forbes* magazine, most people fail to meet their monthly expenses within the first year after they retire. Many retirees fail because they didn't have a plan or specific goals before they retired. Be careful not to fall into that same trap. You can head off the biggest fear by saving enough money to retire comfortably.

#211. What are some important issues that I need to consider before I retire?

Health insurance. What will you do to cover yourself with health insurance until you reach the Medicare age of sixty-five? Interim health insurance can be a very expensive proposition and you can unfortunately rest assured that the cost of whatever plan you have today will continue to go up every time you renew the policy.

Count the dollars. Make sure you have a solid pension strategy in place and know exactly what you'll need in your retirement plan in order to retire.

Your home. If you own your home and plan to move into a less expensive home as one of your retirement strategies, make sure you earmark the money that you'll save for investments.

Living expenses. Consider how you can lower your living expenses. Do you really need two cars? Do you have to go out to eat as often as you did when you were working? How much can you save by shopping bargains, now that you have the time?

#212. How much money will I need to live on when I retire?

Regardless of where you are in the retirement planning stage (i.e., near-term or long-term), it behooves you to estimate how much income you'll need when you retire. There are dozens of books at your local library that cover every facet of retirement. Almost without exception, they include one or more forms that you fill out to determine your retirement income needs.

By balancing your retirement income needs against the financial resources you'll have in place when you retire, such as social security and your company's pension, you can calculate how much capital you'll need to accumulate to supplement any financial shortfalls you might have. As a rule of thumb, you will probably need income amounting to 70 percent or 80 percent of your current income to retire on. If your home is paid for when you retire, the income percentage drops by at least 20 percent. If you're interested in completing a more complex estimate of what you'll need when you retire, check out *U.S. News & World Report*'s retirement calculator on their website (*www.usnews.com*).

#213. **What are some good sources that I can use to help me prepare for my retirement?**

Many resources are available to help you prepare. Some sources are listed here for your convenience. If you enjoy reading books, try Barnes & Noble's website (*www.barnesandnoble.com*) or Amazon's website (*www.amazon.com*) and browse through their retirement book sections. Make sure you get a copy of David Rye's book *250 Questions You Should Ask Before You Retire*. If you prefer researching online, check out Charles Schwab's site, which will help you develop a retirement plan with their online calculators, tools, and advice. Go to their home page at *www.schwab.com* and click on Advice & Retirement at the top of the menu. This section should help you get started.

#214. **How will major expenses change after I retire?**

Unfortunately, you can expect your health costs to increase as you get older. To cover this issue, make sure you absolutely know what is and is not covered by Medicare and any private insurance you may have. Determine what your part is of any co-pay requirement. Typically, your insurer pays 80 percent and you pay 20 percent. Do not forget to include prescription drug costs in your estimates. Your transportation expenses should go down significantly after you retire. Since you don't have to commute to work, whatever you were spending for gasoline and car maintenance should be substantially lower. If you can get rid of one of your cars, you will save even more.

#215. **Can you give me a quick summary of the tax-sheltered retirement plans that may be available to me?**

The tax laws that regulate retirement plans can change at any time. Use the following retirement table as a guide for planning your retirement. Consult with your accountant about the latest tax regulations before you commit any fund to a specific retirement plan.

Tax-Sheltered Retirement Plans

Name	Who Qualifies	Best For	Maximum Contribution
401(k)	Employees working for profit businesses	Everyone who qualifies	Up to 15 percent of salary or $9,500, whichever is less
403(b)	Employees of nonprofit organizations	Everyone who qualifies	Up to 20 percent of salary or $9,500, whichever is less
IRA (Traditional and Roth)	Anyone with earned income	Those who don't have a pension plan or who have put the maximum into their company plans	Up to $5,000 per individual
SEP	Self-employed employees	Self-employed person who is a sole proprietor	Up to 13 percent of self-employment income or $22,500, whichever is less
Keogh plans	The self-employed and employees of unincorporated small businesses	Small business owner who wants to shelter more than what's allowed by most other plans	20 percent of net self-employment income or $30,000, whichever is less
Annuities	Anyone	Someone who has put the maximum into other retirement plans and won't need the money for 10 years	No limits

#216. What exactly is a traditional IRA and do I need one?

Yes, you need an IRA. IRAs, both traditional and Roth, are one of the few investment options left that allow your earnings to grow, tax-free, until you elect to withdraw some or all of the funds that are in your account. Generally, you should first contribute to employer-sponsored plans such as a 401(k) plan to enjoy their matching contributions before you consider opening an IRA account. Before you open an IRA account, make sure you know the rules. As a general rule, don't even think about tapping the money in your IRA until you are fifty-nine and a half or older. There's a 10 percent early withdrawal penalty and you'll pay income tax on anything you take out of the account. If you become totally disabled or need the money to pay for medical expenses, the IRS waives the early withdrawal penalties. Check the regulations first before you make any withdrawals. There are literally thousands of ways to set up an IRA account (see website in the Appendix). If you want to invest IRA funds in CDs, then go to a bank. If you want to invest in mutual funds or stocks, contact a mutual fund company directly or see a stockbroker.

#217. What are Roth IRAs, and how are they different from traditional IRAs?

The major differences between a Roth IRA and a traditional IRA are in the way in which they are funded and in the rules governing withdrawing funds from them. Roth IRAs are funded with your income dollars after taxes have been withdrawn. Traditional IRAs are funded with your income dollars before taxes have been withdrawn. Consequently, you are not taxed on any funds that you withdraw from a Roth IRA. And you can withdraw funds from a Roth IRA at any time, regardless of your age, without incurring a penalty. With a traditional IRA, you're taxed on withdrawals. This is not necessarily a bad thing, since your tax rate may be lower when you retire. You must start withdrawals from a traditional IRA by age seventy and a half.

#218. What is a self-directed IRA?

Self-directed IRAs are set up so that you choose and manage the investments in your account yourself. Most brokers and mutual funds offer them. They may have a small annual fee (usually $50 or less per year) that they charge for this service. Most self-directed IRAs offer a wide variety of investment options for you to consider. To open an IRA account, contact your financial institution or mutual fund representative. If you want to learn more about self-directed IRAs, go to *www.selfdirectedira.org*.

#219. How can I use my home to anchor my retirement plan?

Although many of us stepped into our homes deep in debt years ago, thanks to inflation, we've ended up with an asset that's worth a lot more than what we paid for it. Over the last three decades, the rise in single-family home prices has become the cornerstone of affluence for many Americans. The opportunity to leverage the equity they've built up in their homes has become the foundation of their retirement plan. As you approach retirement, you may want to trade down and move into a smaller home. Before you do that, estimate your profit before you consider selling. What will it cost for an acceptable replacement? If the potential profit from selling your home is minimal, it might not be worth the effort of trading down. Time the sale of your home to take advantage of tax breaks. If you or your spouse is fifty-five or older, you can exclude from taxes up to $500,000 of the capital gains on the sale of your home. If your gain exceeds $500,000 you may also be able to defer tax on the rest by reinvesting in a new residence. Check out all of the tax angles with your accountant before you sell.

#220. How much social security income will I get when I retire?

As a general rule, social security will cover about 25 percent of your preretirement income (less if you're rich, more if you're poor). Social security uses a formula to calculate what is called your Average Indexed Monthly Earnings (AIME) at retirement. Currently, your payment is based on 90 percent of the first $592 of your monthly income, 32 percent of the next $2,975, and then 15 percent of the amount over $3,567. The maximum monthly benefit you can receive at age sixty-five is $1,874 per month.

Your social security income is tax-free unless you are married and your annual earnings are more than $32,000 or single with earnings exceeding $25,000, including half of your social security income in that total. The percentage of your social security that's taxable grows as your adjusted gross income grows. A maximum of 85 percent will be taxable if your adjusted annual income on a joint return reaches $44,000 ($35,000 for singles).

#221. Can I count on getting anything out of social security?

Despite what you may hear in the news, yes, you can. Every year, call the Social Security Administration (800-772-1213) and ask them to send you form SSA-7004 for your personal earnings and benefits estimate. Start checking their records against your annual W-2 forms to make sure they recorded every dollar you paid into social security. Yes, when all of the "baby boomers" retire, the social security system will be financially strained and the federal government has been borrowing heavily from the fund to finance the national debt. However, the government is determined to keep the program.

#222. What can I do now to have my finances in order before I retire?

As you begin to eliminate each component of your debt load, use the debt-free money to begin to max out your retirement accounts (IRAs, 401(k) plans, etc.).

If you are fifty or older, you can start taking advantage of what is called catch-up contributions, which allow you to contribute an extra $5,000 to your 401(k) and an extra $1,000 to a Roth IRA. That's a total of $20,000 through your employee 401(k) contribution of $15,000 and an additional $5,000 for your catch-up contribution. You can also have up to $5,000 for a Roth IRA by adding $4,000 from your Roth IRA rollover to the $1,000 from your catch-up Roth IRA contribution. If you don't have a Roth IRA or 401(k) account, consider opening one.

As if saving for retirement wasn't hard enough, using the money you've saved will present you with a new set of challenges. As a general rule, tap your tax-deferred accounts last. It usually makes sense to withdraw money from your taxable accounts (stocks, mutual fund, etc.) first and let your tax-deferred accounts, such as your IRA, continue to grow as long as possible. You're required to begin withdrawing funds from traditional IRA and 401(k) plans when you turn seventy and a half. There are no mandatory withdrawal requirements for Roth IRAs.

PART **IV**

Putting It All Together

Chapter **23**

ASSEMBLING YOUR FINANCIAL PLAN

A financial plan consolidates into a single plan everything that you have learned and want to do up to this point. All of the notes that you've taken on spending less, consolidating debt, reducing what you're spending on insurance, and the wealth of other debt-related topics that we've covered can be assembled into a binder or file folder so that the material is at your fingertips when you need it. You'll see how to assemble your financial plan in this chapter.

#223. **It seems like everything I try to do to get out of debt requires a plan. Why do I need a financial plan?**

You need a financial plan because it is your starting point for getting out of debt. In all probability, you did not get into debt overnight. It took time and happened because of a number of financial decisions that you made. Unfortunately, your debt won't just go away with a wish and a prayer. It's going to take planning and hard work to make that happen.

#224. **What are the essential components of a financial plan?**

Include a list of specific financial objectives in the front of your plan. For example, it might include a college education for one of your kids, a down payment on a home, or an emergency savings plan. Place dividers in your planning binder for the following sections:

Income Plan: Here is where you show your monthly take-home pay and any sources of additional income that you might have.

Spending Plan: This section includes your monthly budget supplemented with a written spending plan that shows how you will meet specific expense categories and control your expenses.

Saving Plan: What you plan to save each month is shown in your saving plan. Show where the money will come from and how it will be deposited into your savings account(s).

Security Plan: Identify each insurance policy that you have, what is covered, and when the premium payments are due. Include any notes you may have to reduce or increase your insurance premiums.

Tax Plan: Identify the steps that you are planning to take to reduce taxes. Outline the tax deductions that you intend to take and what rate you're in.

Retirement Plan: Contributions that you are making into retirement accounts like IRAs are identified in this section, which will complete your investment plan.

#225. **Who can I call on to objectively review my plan before I implement it?**

After you've put your financial plan together, you are ready for a "critical evaluation" of your plan. If you haven't documented your plan in writing, complete with spreadsheets that project income and expenses throughout your life, then you don't have a plan that's worth considering. When you are confident that you have a solid plan, have it reviewed by a professional, such as a CPA, accountant, or certified financial planner. Of course, this review will cost you money up-front. However, think about it as a small price to pay to ensure that your plan is solid and tight. It's okay to include contingency plans in your master plan if certain assumptions that you have made don't work out. In fact, if you don't have lots of contingencies built into your plan, you probably don't have a solid plan.

#226. Do I need to have professionals review specific sections of my financial plan after I have implemented it?

Yes. If you have a question or need advice on your financial plan, you may want to consult one of the following professionals:

Accountant—for tax advice and tax strategies.

Insurance agent—for insurance coverage issues and policy information.

Stockbroker or mutual fund agent—for investing in stocks and bonds. They can also provide you with information pertaining to money market funds.

Banker—for information on savings and certificate of deposit accounts.

Financial planner—for general advice on finances including the spending, saving, insurance, and investment sections of your financial plan.

#227. What exactly is a financial planner?

A good financial planner is a one-stop money consultant. They in theory know a little something about everything in the financial planning field. They can help you uncover the problems that caused your past debt, help you formulate new financial goals, and develop an implementation plan. They can also help you merge your savings into an investment plan. A majority of planners make their living selling insurance policies, tax-deferred annuities, mutual funds, stocks, and their consultation time. Many financial planners do tax returns.

#228. How do I find a good financial planner?

You can obtain a directory of the financial planners who are in your area by contacting (1) The National Association of Personal Financial Advisors (800-555-6659 or *www.napfa.org*), (2) The American Institute of Certified Public Accountants Personal Financial Division (800-862-4272 or *http://pfp.aicpa.org/resources*), or (3) The Financial Planning Association (800-282-7526 or *www.fpanet.org*). When you begin to make your initial screening calls for a planner, let them know as specifically as you can why you're seeking help and ask them what services they offer. Listen carefully to their answers to help you determine if they have the expertise you need. Ask them for the names of at least three clients whom you can contact who have been with them for at least two years, and make sure you contact these clients to determine their level of satisfaction. Ask the planner how they are paid. They should be willing to disclose all of their compensation requirements in detail. If they won't do this, scratch them off your list and proceed to your next candidate.

#229. How does an estate plan fit into my financial plan?

An estate plan arranges the distribution of assets in your estate when you die or if you become incapacitated. It can be used to make your wishes known in regard to your finances and personal care. Most estate planning begins with a will, which specifies who gets your property when you die. A living will is a supplemental document to a will. It allows you to spell out the medical treatment you want under specific circumstances. For example, you can specify whether you want life-support equipment under certain medical conditions so that your family members don't have to make the difficult decision on your behalf. Your estate plan is the final component of your financial plan. It's your assurance that everything you have worked for all your life will be distributed to your loved ones, according to your wishes.

#230. Where can I find out more about estate planning?

One of the following excellent books on estate planning will get you started:

The 250 Estate Planning Questions Everyone Should Ask by Lita Epstein (Adams Media)

60-Minute Estate Planner by Sandy F. Kraemer (AMACOM Publishing)

Estate Planning for Dummies by Jordan S. Simon and N. Brian Caverly (Wiley Publishing)

Estate Planning Basics by Denis Clifford (Nolo)

#231. Where does a will fit into the scheme of things and do I need one?

Everybody needs a will, whether you are single or married, young or old, healthy or sick. By organizing your estate to your best advantage, you can ensure that your hard-earned money stays in the family or goes to the people and organizations of your choice. A will not only instructs your survivors about how to distribute your property; it also enables you to nominate a guardian to care for your children should they become orphaned. You designate someone whom you trust to act as your estate's executor (e.g., your spouse). This person will be responsible for paying off your creditors and taxes, and ultimately splitting your estate among your heirs in accordance with the wishes you document in your will.

#232. **How do I go about creating a will?**

When you create your will, consider using an estate-planning attorney to help draft the document. You can draft one from do-it-yourself personal computer software, but any savings you may incur over attorney fees are hardly worth the risk of a mistake or oversight on your part. If you prefer to write your own will, you should do so only if your will is not complicated. Quicken offers a software product called WillMaker that is available at computer stores and online (*www.nolo.com*).

Chapter 24

BECOMING FINANCIALLY INDEPENDENT

Taking on the task of getting yourself out of debt is going to present you with some tough challenges, as have been addressed throughout this book. If you are serious about making it happen, then you need to establish a goal that comes from your heart—one that will give you the drive to make it happen. How about setting a goal of becoming financially independent? That sounds good, but what does that mean?

Becoming financially independent means you have secured sources of income that will support a lifestyle that's acceptable to you for the rest of your life without having to rely on borrowed money. In this chapter, you will learn what you need to do to become financially independent.

#233. Becoming financially independent sounds great. Why do most people fail to make it happen?

Financial independence is a goal that we all would like to achieve at some stage of our lives. Financial independence is as much of a state of mind as it is money. Lots of us spend all kinds of time thinking and talking about how we are going to achieve it, but few of us are willing to actually take any action to make it happen.

#234. What resources can I turn to that will show me how to become financially independent?

There are some excellent resources that are offered at a minimal cost or free to anyone who is interested. A great website that offers a variety of articles pertaining to financial freedom is *www.money. cnn.com*. It may also be worthwhile to consider a subscription to a monthly magazine such as *Kiplinger's Personal Finance Magazine* or *Money*. It can be a helpful reminder to keep you on your financial track when you receive the magazine every month through your mail. Of course, books on this topic are plentiful and can be checked out at your local library for free or ordered used and at a discounted price through *www.amazon.com*. A couple of suggested books are *The 9 Steps to Financial Freedom* by Suze Orman or *The Six-Day Financial Makeover* by Robert Pagliarini.

#235. What basic steps do I need to go through to become financially independent?

Save and invest your money. You need a savings plan that is flexible but firm, and, most important, is something you can stick to. Your first challenge will be to get control over your spending habits and establish a monthly budget for everything you buy. If you can start saving on even the little things, it will add up to big dollars over a relatively short period of time.

Set financial goals. To be meaningful, a goal must be very specific, with a designated completion date assigned to it. Start with small, relatively simple financial goals such as opening a savings account this week. As you become more comfortable in the goal-setting process, move up to intermediate goals like making regular monthly deposits into your IRA.

Avoid unnecessary debt. If, for example, you want to take a cruise to Alaska but you don't have the money, wait until you do. If you don't have the money, don't use credit cards to get it.

Buy a home and invest wisely. It is one of the best tax shelters you can get. Pay off your home mortgage faster by sending your payment coupons in early along with an extra payment. Make sure you state to the lender that payment goes toward the principal.

Drive a car that's paid for. There is nothing better than a car that's paid for. Don't rush out to trade it in just because the loan is paid off. If Old Faithful is still running, keep it and save the money.

#236. I have heard that if you really want to become financially independent, you have to invest your money. Why?

You want your hard-earned money to continue to grow and prosper. To do that, you need to begin building an investment portfolio that encompasses your goals and time horizon. Your ultimate goal may be to become financially independent. How soon you want to make that happen and in what standard of living style can significantly affect your decisions on how you invest your money. How you choose to diversify (e.g., stocks, bonds, mutual funds) depends on your rate-of-return goals, how much risk you can tolerate, and how long you can invest your money.

#237. What are the basic types of investments that I should consider?

Money magazine's website has a feature called Money 101. Lesson 4 (found at *http://money.cnn.com/magazines/moneymag/money101/lesson4*) walks you through the basics about investment types and what you need to know. There are stocks, bonds, notes, and funds, just to name a few of the types of investments that are covered. This site is a great place to start to understand your different investment options and what to look out for. You will need to review each investment option in detail to help you determine the right strategy for you.

#238. **How do you define rate of return and what should I expect from my investments?**

Rate of return (ROR) is a measure of the money an investor makes when he invests in something like a stock or an antique clock. It is typically reflected as an annualized percentage increase of what you sold an investment for over what you paid for it. For example, if you purchased a share of stock for $100 and sold it one year later for $110, you would have enjoyed a 10 percent ROR profit ($110/$100 = 1.10). If you purchased a share of stock for $110 and sold it one year later for $100, you would have a 9 percent ROR loss ($100/$110 = .90). A positive ROR is an investor's reward for the risk he has taken to make an investment. High-risk investments demand higher rates of return. At a minimum, you should expect an ROR that exceeds 5 percent because you can easily get that through a "no risk" money market fund.

#239. **Can you give me a summary of the investments that I should consider as I begin to get out of debt?**

Investment Options

Investment Type	Risk Level	Investments Made	Objectives
Money Market Funds	Low	Commercial paper such as CDs and treasury notes	Earn short-term interest rates from secure investments
Bonds	Low to Medium	Government and corporate bonds with mature dates of between 1 and 15 years	Speculates on low interest rates to get higher returns at maturity
Individual Stocks	Medium to High	Select stocks to match the performance of a specific market	Follow higher average market return
Mutual Funds	Medium to High	Invest in corporate stocks, bonds, and commodities	Looks for stocks, bonds, and commodities with reliable performance over time

#240. **What are mutual funds and should I consider investing in them?**

Mutual funds have become an extremely popular way to invest for people who don't have the time to conduct their own investment analysis. Today, there are thousands of funds to choose from with a vast range of investment and diversification options, from ultra-conservative bond funds to aggressive stock funds that specialize in fast-growth companies. When you invest in a mutual fund, you're buying shares in a portfolio of securities managed by a professional investment firm. Some funds specialize in only one type of security or industry, while others invest in a variety of securities to minimize risk. And not all funds invest in stocks. Many specialize in the bond market and commodities, and the international markets as well. Your rate of return depends on how well the portfolio of securities is doing at any one time. The key advantages of mutual funds are summarized as follows:

Diversification. When you invest in a fund, your money is riding on a large number of securities instead of just a few, which lessens the risk.

Low cost management. Professional management fees typically run around 1 percent of your investment annually. You can sell your mutual funds any time, just like a stock.

Flexibility. If you've invested in one of the funds offered by a company like Fidelity Investments, which offers its investors a family of funds, you can switch between the funds in the family as market conditions or your investment objectives change, at no additional cost.

#241. **How do I find a good mutual fund and how are they bought and sold?**

There are over a thousand mutual funds to choose from, so finding the one that is right for you can be a tedious task. Here's how to quickly go about finding the better funds:

Read up. There are a number of books out there that specialize in investing in funds. For example, *Morningstar Guide to Mutual Funds: Five-Star Strategies for Success* by Christine Benz gives you a quick roundup of investment tips.

Use research tools. *Barron's* magazine and the *Wall Street Journal* publish fund performance data. Don't ignore the ads in newspapers and financial magazines. Fund companies like to advertise their better-performing funds.

Use the Internet. To start you off, *www.morningstar.com*, *www.kiplinger.com*, and *www.investools.com* are three sites that can help you select funds that meet your parameters.

Typically, you can buy or sell funds directly through your fund company. However, if the funds were purchased through another source, such as a third-party broker, you can go directly to them, but you will most likely incur a sales charge. To avoid any charges, several financial organizations—e.g., Schwab's OneSource, Vanguard's FundAccess, and Fidelity's FundsNetwork—offer no-charge options.

#242. Whenever I open a financial magazine, I see an article about the value of starting to invest early in life. What are they talking about?

Most of those articles are written to illustrate a point. For example, let's suppose that twin brothers each decided to invest $1,000 a year in a mutual fund at age twenty. One brother decides to stop contributing annually at age thirty. The other brother continues contributing until they both retire at sixty. On average, the fund earned 10 percent annually. How much would each twin have accumulated when he reached age sixty? $450,000 and $1,800,000, respectively, which illustrates the value of getting out of debt and investing early in life.

#243. **Are there any safe investments that I can make?**

There are several investments for you to consider that are as safe as money in the bank. And they all offer interest rates that are substantially better than what you'll get in traditional savings accounts.

Insured money market funds are pools of money that are invested in short-term debts issued by the government, the nation's most creditworthy companies, or banks. They are partly insured by private insurance companies. Check with your broker to find out what "partly" means. You can buy money market funds through your broker for as little as $500, and many forms carry check-writing privileges.

Certificates of deposits are one of the safest investments you can make since they are insured for up to $100,000. You can buy them from banks and credit unions. The price of most CDs start at $500 and go up from there. They are designed to mature at different lengths of time and offer rates that fluctuate daily. Shop around for the best rates in your area or check Bank Rate Monitor's website (*www.bankrate.com*) for current rates.

U.S. Savings Bonds can be purchased for as little as $25 each. If you use them for college expenses, the interest they earn is tax free. Some employers offer them through payroll deduction plans, or you can purchase them through savings and loan associations.

Chapter **25**

STAYING AHEAD OF THE GAME

Congratulations—you have made it to the final chapter in the book. You're not done however, because steering clear of debt and building financial independence is a lifelong endeavor. The key to your ongoing success is keeping your head above water and staying ahead of the game. This chapter addresses several important issues that will help you make the right financial decisions and protect what you have built.

#244. We all want to stay ahead in the money management game. What does that mean, anyway?

Debt is a tough opponent to play against. It has beaten more good people than we will ever know about. You are now at the end of *The 250 Questions You Should Ask to Get Out of Debt*, and if it helped you eliminate all your debt along the way, congratulations. If you are not yet out of debt, but you were able to free up some cash and put it where it will do you the most good, then you are winning the game, but you're still in it. Just remember that managing your money is an ongoing necessity to achieve your goals. If you continue to make good financial decisions, and develop good spending, saving, and investment habits, you will be the ultimate winner.

#245. **What is the key to staying out of debt?**

The key ingredient is making your money last. If you have religiously gone through the previous 244 questions, you should understand by now how important a financial plan is to help you get out of debt. However, once you get out of debt, do not discard your plan. You'll need it to make sure you stay out of debt and continue to invest your money so that it will last you a lifetime.

#246. **Do I need separate funds to cover financial emergencies?**

The emergency fund is the most important savings category that you can have. It is created to cover expenses related to emergencies such as the loss of a job, unexpected medical expenses, car repairs, or other crisis situations that cost money. It should be an important part of your financial plan because the last thing you want is to be forced to go back into debt to cover emergency expenses. How much you need in emergency reserves depends on you. A minimum of three months' salary is recommended. Set a monetary target and begin making deposits into a separate savings account for this purpose. Short-term savings funds are used for planned expenses and emergency expenses. Regular recurring contributions are essential to assure that your "nest egg" builds at a consistent rate. Long-term savings are typically invested in equities that can provide long-term growth.

#247. **Do I need insurance to cover financial emergencies?**

Failing to protect your financial well-being without adequate insurance is like jumping out of an airplane without a parachute. You will eventually hit the ground. The question is, how hard do you want to hit it? Your emergency fund plan should include a list of insurance policies you currently have, complete with policy numbers, the amount of coverage, and what exactly is covered. Identify any policies where you believe coverage needs to be increased, decreased, or eliminated. Next, list any additional insurance coverage you may need (e.g., medical insurance) and set a date as to when you'll get it. Review the insurance part of your financial plan at least every six months to keep it current with any changes in your life.

#248. **What advice can you give me that will help me stay on track to get out of debt?**

Living a frugal or even a goal-oriented life is difficult in America, where every time you turn around, advertisers are encouraging you to spend more. It may be helpful to you to find others or a group in your area who share your get-out-of-debt goals. A good place to start your search on the Internet is at *www.simpleliving.net*. You might want to also investigate Debtors Anonymous (*www.debt orsanonymous.org*), which is a twelve-step program designed to help people kick their addiction to overspending. The site also includes invaluable information about ways to save money.

#249. **Will it all be worth it once I gain control over my personal finances?**

As you begin to take over your debt, your wealth will grow. You'll be able to retire even more of your debt and for the first time begin to feel in control of your money. But, no matter how carefully you plan or how committed you are to your goals, stuff can happen.

You can lose a job, suffer an illness, or be thrown off-track in any number of ways that can disrupt your ability to reach some of your goals. If that happens, be prepared to rethink your goals and implement a new plan. That's all part of the game, and if you get discouraged, just remember that winners are the ones who never give up.

#250. **Can you summarize all of the advice that you have given me into a few concise paragraphs?**

This book started out by showing you multiple ways to save money. Why? Because you should have some extra money that you could invest in the wide variety of investment vehicles covered throughout the book. Making, saving, and investing money the smart way takes discipline, time, and patience. If you're not willing to do that, you'll never achieve financial independence. The irony is that it really doesn't take much effort to become financially secure if you are willing to practice self-discipline now, for future peace of mind and prosperity.

If you start with a financial plan, a solid set of financial goals, and work out from there, you will become financially independent. As you begin to climb out of debt, invest your money wisely. Set up and religiously deposit money into a savings account. Make sure that you have an emergency fund so that you can pay for emergency expenses instead of charging them on credit cards.

Develop a basic understanding of investment options like stocks, mutual funds, bonds, and money market funds. As you begin to save money, invest it in securities that fit with where you want to go financially. Use debit cards instead of credit cards. Debit cards draw money from your checking account to pay for a purchase. They don't allow you to overspend the way credit cards do. Place your credit cards in a safe, out-of-the-way place and use them only for legitimate financial emergencies. Buy and keep a home and drive a car that's paid for.

In conclusion, it is sincerely hoped that all of the get-out-of-debt ideas covered in this book will help you keep more of what you have today and achieve the financial success tomorrow that you deserve. We want to wish you the very best in your efforts toward achieving financial independence.

APPENDIX OF RESOURCES BY SUBJECT

Advice Books on Debt

If you need more advice on reducing your debt, try Barnes & Noble's website (*www.barnesandnoble.com*) or Amazon.com's website (*www.amazon.com*) and browse through their debt-related books.

Some of the better get-out-of-debt books to consider are summarized as follows:

Deal with Your Debt by Liz Weston (Pearson Education, 2005)

Pay It Down! by Jean Chatzky (Penguin Group, 2006)

The Road to Wealth by Suze Orman (Penguin Group, 2008)

The 250 Personal Finance Questions Everyone Should Ask by Peter Sander (Adams Media, 2005)

Budgeting

You can view a sample budget at *www.personalbudgeting.com*.

A good resource and tool for developing a budget is available at *www.simpleplanning.net*.

College Expenses

To learn more about federal financial aid and how to apply, visit the U.S. Department of Education's website at *www.ed.gov*.

Credit Cards

To find out about credit card options, visit *www.e-wisdom.com*.

The website at *www.cardratings.com* offers a variety of resources to help you understand everything related to credit cards.

Credit Score

For a fee, you can find out what your score is at *www.myfico.com*.

You can check your credit report at all three bureaus at *www.annualcreditreport.com*.

Debt Assessment

The website at *http://cgi.money.cnn.com/tools/debtplanner/debtplanner.jsp* will help you project when you will be debt free.

If you are interested in learning more about bankruptcy, go to *www.bankruptcyinfo.com*.

Estate Planning

If you want to create a basic will on your computer, Quicken offers a software product called WillMaker that is available in computer stores and at *www.nolo.com*.

Financial Planners

The American Institute of Certified Public Accountants (*www.aicpa.org*)
Personal Financial Planning Division, 1211 Avenue of the Americas, New York, NY 10036, 800-862-4272

The National Association of Personal Financial Advisors (*www.napfa.org*)
355 W. Dunbee Rd., Suite 200, Buffalo Grove, IL 60089, 800-333-6659

Financial Planning

Quicken.com offers a Debt Reduction Planner, an excellent tool for about $50.

A website that offers a variety of articles pertaining to financial planning is at *www.money.cnn.com.*

Insurance

If you are paying for your own insurance, go to *www.ehealthinsurance.com* to determine if there is a less expensive plan to switch to.

The website at *www.nmfn.com* will help you estimate your life span and need for life insurance based on your age, gender, lifestyle, and medical history.

Investment Brokers

Charles Schwab (*www.schwab.com*)

Fidelity Investments (*www.fidelity.com*)

T. Rowe Price (*www.troweprice.com*)

Vanguard Group (*www.vanguard.com*)

Investment Resources

The websites at *www.morningstar.com*, *www.kiplinger.com*, and *www.investools.com* will help you select stocks and mutual funds that meet your investment parameters.

Shop around for the best certificate of deposit rates in your area at *www.bankrate.com.*

Loans

To learn more about home loans, foreclosure prevention, and predatory lending, go to *www.loansafe.org.*

Bankrate.com can find the best rates available in your area for motor vehicles.

Motor Vehicles

For comprehensive car-buying information, go to *www.edmunds* *.com*, *www.autobytel.com*, and *www.carsmart.com*.

To get an estimate of used car values, go to the Kelly Blue Book at *www.kbb.com*, Edmunds at *www.edmunds.com*, or eAuto at *www.eauto.com*.

If you are interested in purchasing a used vehicle, check out Trader Online (*www.traderonline.com*), Kelley Blue Book's Classifieds (*www.kbb.com*), Online Auto (*www.onlineauto.com*), or Auto Web Interactive (*www.autoweb.com*).

If you are interested in purchasing a new vehicle, check out *www.autosite.com* to find dealer invoice prices or find out about the maintenance records on cars that interest you.

Real Estate

Cost-of-living and moving calculators are available at *http://cgi* *.money.cnn.com/tools*.

To calculate mortgage rates and review *Money* magazine articles on real estate, go to *www.usatoday.com/money*.

Retirement

Charles Schwab's website will help you develop a retirement plan with their online calculators, tools, and advice at *www.schwab.com* (click on Advice & Retirement at the top of the menu).

Quicken offers a software product called WillMaker that is available at several computer stores and online at *www.nolo.com*.

A retirement budget worksheet is available at *www.fidelity.com* when you select the Retirement & Guidance option in their main menu.

A retirement calculator can be accessed at *www.usnews.com* when you select the Retirement sub-menu that is under their Money & Business main menu.

If you are interested in getting an annuity quote, go to *www* *.immediateannuities.com*.

Saving Money

For steps to take to save money, go to *www.themoneykeys.com.*

To determine if you are saving enough, go to *www.kiplinger .com.*

Shopping and Selling

If you are selling a household item that would be difficult to get an appraisal on, see what similar items are selling for in the classified advertisements or on *www.ebay.com, www.netmarket.com,* or *www .craigslist.com.*

Yellow Page listings are available at *http://search.bigfoot.com* or *www.switchboard.com.*

Taxes

For tax deductions, go to *www.bottomlinesecrets.com/extra.*

For tax preparation ideas, go to *http://tax.yahoo.com/checklist .html.*

Travel Sites

www.expedia.com

www.travelocity.com

www.bestfares.com

www.budgettravel.com

Web Search Engines

Alta Vista: *www.altavista.com*

Google: *www.google.com*

HotBot: *www.hotbot.com*

Lycos: *www.lycos.com*

Yahoo!: *www.yahoo.com*

THE 250 QUESTIONS

CHAPTER 1 DEALING WITH YOUR DEBT

#1. What is the primary cause of personal debt?

#2. Exactly what is personal debt and how does it affect my credit?

#3. How do I determine if I have a serious debt problem?

#4. What do people who get into debt have in common?

#5. Why do a lot of people fail to ever get out of debt?

#6. Why am I paying more for a loan just because I owe more than what I should?

#7. Is bankruptcy a good alternative way to get out of debt?

#8. Is there such a thing as good debt?

#9. What can I do now to begin getting out of debt?

#10. What is a spending plan and do I need one?

#11. If I decide to set up and maintain a spending plan, what will it help me accomplish?

CHAPTER 2 DETERMINING WHERE YOU WANT TO GO

#12. How do I start to understand my debts?

#13. How do I determine where I am and where I want to go financially?

#14. What are some of the steps I can take to reduce my expenses?

#15. What are some of the areas that I need to consider to make some extra money?

#16. What is a financial planner, and do I need one?

#17. Will inflation help me get out of debt?

#18. How might my financial outlook change as I get older?

#19. Do banks have money management counselors who are worth talking to?

#20. Are there questionable get-out-of-debt deals that I should avoid?

#21. Is my standard of living disrupting my ability to get out of debt?

#22. What can I do to motivate myself to get out of debt?

CHAPTER 3 LIVING ON A BUDGET

#23. What is the difference between a budget and a spending plan?

#24. What are the primary components of a monthly budget?

#25. What are the five steps that I need to take in preparing a budget?

#26. Does my budget need to be in writing?

#27. Why do people fail to stay within their budget?

#28. Why do people buy a lot of stuff that they really don't need?

#29. How can I get my spouse and family to commit to a monthly budget?

#30. What's the best way to maintain a budget?

#31. What should I do if I spend more than what's in my budget?

#32. My friend tells me that if you borrow what you need, you don't need a budget. What exactly does that mean?

CHAPTER 4 AVOIDING DEBT TRAPS

#33. What are the most common debt traps?

#34. I'm spending every dime I make. What can I do to get my expenses in line with what I make?

#35. Are there immediate steps that I can take now to stop borrowing?

#36. What are the symptoms of a bad loan?

#37. How can I figure out what a loan really costs?

#38. Should I consider a rent-to-own deal?

#39. Are loans secured by my car's title a debt trap?

#40. What are refund anticipation loans?

#41. What can I do to avoid foreclosure?

#42. Should I avoid the get-out-of-debt schemes that come my way?

CHAPTER 5 CHECKING YOUR CREDIT SCORE

#43. Exactly what is a credit score, and how is it used?

#44. Who do I contact to find out what my credit score is?

#45. What can I do to improve my credit score?

#46. How does bankruptcy affect one's credit score?

#47. If I disagree with anything that's on my credit report, what action can I take?

#48. What is a good credit score and what can it do for me?

CHAPTER 6 CONSOLIDATING DEBTS

#49. How should the interest rates that I'm paying on my debts affect my decision to consolidate?

#50. How do I get started implementing a consolidation plan?

#51. I have some equity in my home. What are home equity loans all about?

#52. When does it pay to refinance your mortgage?

#53. How do I figure out which debts to pay off first?

#54. Are there any consolidation scam schemes that I should avoid?

#55. Should I consider switching from one credit card to another credit card?

CHAPTER 7 SPENDING LESS

#56. What can I do to control my urge to always spend money?

#57. How do I create a "spend-less" plan?

#58. What is the best way to get my family to participate in my spend-less plan?

#59. What are some ways that I can cut back on gasoline for my car?

#60. I'm spending a lot of money each month on home energy bills. How can I cut back?

#61. I'm considering refinancing my home. How should I do it?

#62. Is there any way I can reduce my monthly house payment without having to refinance?

#63. I have accumulated $10,000 in credit card debt. What should I do?

#64. I rent. What can I do to keep my rent from always going up?

#65. What are some ways to save when I shop for food?

#66. Is it worth my while to try to reduce the interest rate I'm paying?

CHAPTER 8 MAKING HARD CHOICES

#67. What are some of the hard choices that I need to consider to get out of debt?

#68. Who should I see who can help me decide what hard choices I need to make?

#69. Should I consider selling my home?

#70. Is my car sabotaging my ability to make ends meet?

#71. Should I really consider getting rid of all my credit cards?

#72. I am totally unable to save money. How can I change my ways?

#73. I own some valuable assets that I don't need or want. How can I determine what to sell them for?

#74. Should I consider bankruptcy to get out of debt, or are there alternatives?

#75. If I decide to declare bankruptcy, how do I apply?

#76. How much does it cost to declare bankruptcy?

#77. Who can I consult to help me determine if I should declare bankruptcy?

#78. Do I need credit counseling and support?

Part 2 Finding Money

CHAPTER 9 PAYING YOURSELF FIRST

#79. What does "paying yourself first" mean?

#80. Can I lower the amount of taxes that are withheld from my paycheck as a way of paying myself first?

#81. Where should I put the money that I pay myself?

#82. Should I use the money I pay myself for savings or paying off debt first?

#83. What is a simple way of paying myself first?

#84. Okay, I got the concept that's behind the paying-yourself-first idea. What are some things that I can do to make it a part of my daily plan?

#85. As soon as I pay myself, I spend the money. What can I do?

#86. Why are you making a big deal out of the pay-yourself-first exercises?

CHAPTER 10 SEARCHING FOR HIDDEN MONEY

#87. Where do I start my search to find hidden money?

#88. What are five sources of money that I should look at first?

#89. I have a friend who keeps telling me that buying used is better than buying new. Do you agree?

#90. I'm responsible for paying back student loans that cost me a lot each month. What can I do to reduce my monthly loan payments?

#91. Should I consider getting a cheaper car?

#92. My monthly car payment is a killer. What can I do to bring it down to earth?

#93. What are equity lines, and are they a viable source of money?

#94. How much money do I need to find to get out of debt?

#95. How can I keep myself motivated to keep looking for money to get out of debt?

#96. There have got to be ways to reduce what I'm paying for insurance. Can you help me find some hidden money in my insurance premiums?

#97. Do I need to keep track of everything I'm doing to find money?

CHAPTER 11 USING HOME EQUITY

#98. I have a lot of equity in my home. Should I keep my house or sell it?

#99. Is a reverse mortgage an option that I should consider?

#100. Who makes home equity loans, and what are the costs and risks?

#101. When does it make sense to consider a home equity loan?

#102. Should I borrow against the equity in my home to finance college for my kids?

#103. My friends tell me that there are a number of financial benefits that are attached to home equity. What are they?

#104. What questions should I ask myself before I take out a home equity loan?

#105. Should I sell my home, use the equity to pay off debt, and rent or buy a cheaper home?

#106. Why is it wise to repay equity loans on time and without fail?

#107. How does home equity fit into my retirement plan?

CHAPTER 12 PAYING COLLEGE EXPENSES

#108. I have a child who wants to go to college. How can I determine what it will cost?

#109. Are there some tax-free ways to save for college?

#110. Are there preferred loans available to help me pay for my child's college?

#111. What exactly is college financial aid and how can I apply?

#112. How can I determine if I qualify for financial aid?

#113. How do I apply for federal college financial aid?

#114. Who can help me learn more about financial aid?

#115. Do the individual colleges and state governments offer financial aid?

#116. Where are the best places to find college scholarships?

#117. Are there ways to pay for college on an installment plan?

CHAPTER 13 CONTROLLING CREDIT CARDS

#118. What's the difference between a debit card and a credit card?

#119. What is the primary purpose of credit cards?

#120. What are the different types of credit cards and hidden costs of using them?

#121. What are the different types of fees charged by credit cards, and which one is best for me?

#122. How do people get into trouble using credit cards?

#123. How can I motivate myself to limit what I'm charging to credit cards?

#124. What are some general guidelines for paying off credit cards?

#125. I'm charging everything to my credit cards. How do I just kick the habit for good?

#126. What will happen to me once I solve my credit card habit?

CHAPTER 14 AVOIDING BAD LOANS

#127. Is there any such thing as a good loan?

#128. What are the symptoms of a bad loan?

#129. What are the three basic types of loans, and what are the advantages and disadvantages of each type?

#130. How do I determine if I have any bad loans?

#131. What are some of the loans that I should avoid at all costs?

#132. What questions should I always ask a lender before I sign the loan papers?

#133. Why should I avoid loans with prepayment penalties?

#134. Is a loan against my retirement account a good idea?

#135. How does my credit score affect the cost of a loan?

#136. What does a lender mean when they say you're "upside down" in your car loan?

#137. How can I avoid getting a car loan that I can't afford?

#138. What alternatives do I have to avoid short-term high-rate loans?

CHAPTER 15 PAYING OFF DEBT

#139. How do I determine which debts I should pay off first?

#140. What payoff solutions should I avoid?

#141. If I don't have the money to pay off high-interest loans, what can I do?

#142. I love my car but my car payment is killing me. What should I do?

#143. What is the primary difference between a fifteen-year and a thirty-year mortgage?

#144. What are the advantages of paying off my mortgage?

#145. Should I consider borrowing money at a lower interest rate to pay off my high interest rate loans?

#146. Are there good websites and software application programs that can help me get out of debt?

CHAPTER 16 GETTING TAX MONEY BACK

#147. Where do I start looking for tax breaks?

#148. What is the Alternative Minimum Tax (AMT) all about, and do I need to be concerned about it?

#149. How can I reduce the amount that gets deducted from my paycheck for taxes?

#150. Is it really worth it to save every receipt that is tax deductible?

#151. How should I store my tax receipts and records?

#152. I'm afraid of the IRS and therefore don't like to prepare my own tax return. Am I overreacting?

#153. How should I plan for my taxes?

#154. How can I deduct what I spend on home improvements when I sell my home?

#155. What are the advantages and disadvantages of having someone prepare my tax return?

#156. Where do I look to find someone to prepare my tax return?

#157. How can I get my money's worth if I elect to have someone prepare my tax return?

#158. How can I reduce my property taxes?

CHAPTER 17 CREATING A SAVINGS PLAN

#159. Where am I going to find any money to save?

#160. I've procrastinated about saving money all of my life. Can you help me get motivated?

#161. In general, how much should people save?

#162. Can you give me five painless ways to start saving some money?

#163. What are passbook savings accounts?

#164. I have heard that Americans on average save less than 1 percent of their income. Why is it so low?

#165. What is a certificate of deposit (CD) and should I consider it as a place to save my money?

#166. What are money market funds and should I consider them as a place to save my money?

#167. I don't have that much to save. Is the interest rate important and where should I put my savings?

#168. What is a good savings strategy to have?

#169. What is compound interest and how does it affect my savings?

Part 3 Improving Your Quality of Life

CHAPTER 18 ACQUIRING A CAR

#170. What questions should I ask before I get a car?

#171. What does it cost to own a car?

#172. How can I get the best car loan possible?

#173. I've decided to get rid of my car. What options and issues should I consider?

#174. What are the advantages of buying a used vehicle?

#175. Should I consider leasing a car?

#176. I'm considering buying a new car. How are they priced?

#177. How do I find an honest and reasonable automotive repair facility?

#178. How can I reduce the cost of my car insurance?

CHAPTER 19 MAKING MORE MONEY

#179. If I decide to moonlight, do I need to let my employer know what I'm doing?

#180. How do I start looking for a second job?

#181. Should I consider quitting my current job and getting one that pays more?

#182. I have always dreamed of starting a home-based business. How can I find out more about them?

#183. How can I make sure that if I start a home business, it will have a good chance of taking off?

CHAPTER 20 BUYING A HOME

#184. Why is a home a smart investment?

#185. What can I afford and what type of home should I buy?

#186. Where can I find bargains on homes?

#187. What are the costs of owning a home versus renting one?

#188. Can I afford to purchase a home?

#189. What should I look for before I buy a home?

#190. Should I buy a condominium instead of a house?

#191. If I decide to move, should I rent or buy a home?

#192. How can I assess a good purchase price on a home?

#193. What do I need to know about mortgages?

#194. How does my FICO score affect my mortgage rate?

#195. Can I shop for a mortgage on the Internet?

CHAPTER 21 PROTECTING YOURSELF WITH INSURANCE

#196. What's the difference between term and whole life insurance, and do I even need life insurance when I'm trying to get out of debt?

#197. How much life insurance do I really need?

#198. Is there any way to save on life insurance premiums?

#199. What do the many categories of auto insurance cover and which ones do I need?

#200. What is disability insurance and do I need it?

#201. Everybody needs health insurance but I can't afford it. What can I do?

#202. What is the best way to shop for affordable health care insurance?

#203. I'm paying a fortune for homeowners insurance. Is there any way I can reduce my premium?

#204. My home is in what they call a low to medium area for floods. Do I need flood insurance?

#205. I've heard that credit insurance is a waste of money. Is it?

#206. Does it make any sense to get dental insurance?

#207. How are insurance deductibles established and how can I use them to my advantage?

#208. Can I get discounts for using the same insurance provider for multiple policies?

CHAPTER 22 THINKING ABOUT RETIRING

#209. Am I ready to retire and can I afford it?

#210. What are the greatest fears people have when they retire?

#211. What are some important issues that I need to consider before I retire?

#212. How much money will I need to live on when I retire?

#213. What are some good sources that I can use to help me prepare for my retirement?

#214. How will major expenses change after I retire?

#215. Can you give me a quick summary of the tax-sheltered retirement plans that may be available to me?

#216. What exactly is a traditional IRA and do I need one?

#217. What are Roth IRAs, and how are they different from traditional IRAs?

#218. What is a self-directed IRA?

#219. How can I use my home to anchor my retirement plan?

#220. How much social security income will I get when I retire?

#221. Can I count on getting anything out of social security?

#222. What can I do now to have my finances in order before I retire?

Part 4 Putting It All Together

CHAPTER 23 ASSEMBLING YOUR FINANCIAL PLAN

#223. It seems like everything I try to do to get out of debt requires a plan. Why do I need a financial plan?

#224. What are the essential components of a financial plan?

#225. Who can I call on to objectively review my plan before I implement it?

#226. Do I need to have professionals review specific sections of my financial plan after I have implemented it?

#227. What exactly is a financial planner?

#228. How do I find a good financial planner?

#229. How does an estate plan fit into my financial plan?

#230. Where can I find out more about estate planning?

#231. Where does a will fit into the scheme of things and do I need one?

#232. How do I go about creating a will?

CHAPTER 24 BECOMING FINANCIALLY INDEPENDENT

#233. Becoming financially independent sounds great. Why do most people fail to make it happen?

#234. What resources can I turn to that will show me how to become financially independent?

#235. What basic steps do I need to go through to become financially independent?

#236. I have heard that if you really want to become financially independent, you have to invest your money. Why?

#237. What are the basic types of investments that I should consider?

#238. How do you define rate of return and what should I expect from my investments?

#239. Can you give me a summary of the investments that I should consider as I begin to get out of debt?

#240. What are mutual funds and should I consider investing in them?

#241. How do I find a good mutual fund and how are they bought and sold?

#242. Whenever I open a financial magazine, I see an article about the value of starting to invest early in life. What are they talking about?

#243. Are there any safe investments that I can make?

CHAPTER 25 STAYING AHEAD OF THE GAME

#244. We all want to stay ahead in the money management game. What does that mean, anyway?

#245. What is the key to staying out of debt?

#246. Do I need separate funds to cover financial emergencies?

#247. Do I need insurance to cover financial emergencies?

#248. What advice can you give me that will help me stay on track to get out of debt?

#249. Will it all be worth it once I gain control over my personal finances?

#250. Can you summarize all of the advice that you have given me into a few concise paragraphs?

INDEX

Adams Businesses You Can Start Almanac, 114

Annuities, 138

Assets, selling, 47

Average Indexed Monthly Earnings (AIME), 140

Bankruptcy, 7–8, 30, 47–49

Banks
  car financing by, 107
  money management counselors, 14–15

Benz, Christine, 156

Bonds, 157

Budget, 6–7, 17–22

Car(s), 105–12
  cost of owning, 106–7
  getting rid of, options, 108
  insurance, 26, 61, 111–12, 128–29
  leasing, 109
  new vs. used, 108–9
  paid for, 153
  pricing of new, 110
  questions to ask before getting, 105–6
  reducing fuel use, 39–40
  reducing spending on, 46, 59, 87
  repair facilities for, 110–11
  selling, 47, 108

Car loans, 8, 11
  avoiding unaffordable, 85
  obtaining best possible, 107
  reducing monthly payments, 59–60
  title/pink slip, 25–26
  upside down, 84–85

Cash-out refinancing, 33, 34

Catch-up contributions, 141

Caverly, N. Brian, 149

Certificates of deposit (CDs), 100, 139, 157

Clifford, Denis, 149

COBRA (Consolidated Omnibus Budget Reconciliation Act), 130

College expenses, 69–74
  determining, 69

  financial aid for, 69, 71–73
  grants for, 71
  home equity for, 66
  installment plan payments, 73–74
  loans for (see Student loans)
  scholarships for, 71, 73
  tax breaks and, 70

The Complete Car Cost Guide, 107

The Complete Idiot's Guide to College Financial Aid (Rye), 73

Condominiums, 120–21

Consolidating debts, 32–36, 86, 88–89

Consumer Credit Counseling Service, 15

Consumer Reports, 108, 110, 111

Credit, 4

Credit cards, 75–79
  average owed on, 3
  budgeting for payments, 18
  cash advances on, 5
  debit cards compared with, 75, 161
  excessive number of, 5
  fees charged by, 77
  getting rid of, 8, 46, 78–79
  guidelines for paying off, 78
  hidden cost of using, 76–77
  inappropriate use of, 5–6
  interest rates on, 11, 76–77, 87
  limiting charges on, 77–78
  primary purpose of, 76
  switching to another, 35–36, 87
  $10,000 or more on, 41
  types of, 76

Credit counseling, 49

Credit score, 7, 28–31, 84

Debit cards, 75, 76, 161

Debt
  commonalities of people into, 5–6
  credit affected by, 4
  defined, 4
  determining seriousness of, 5
  good, 8
  inflation impact on, 14
  key to staying out of, 159

Debt—*continued*
  motivation for getting out of, 16
  paying off, 86–89
  payments to yourself and, 54–55
  payoff solutions to avoid, 87
  primary cause of, 3–4
  prioritizing payments, 35, 86–87
  questionable get-out-of deals, 15, 27
  reasons for failure to escape, 6–7
  standard of living and, 15–16
  total household, 3, 20
  traps, avoiding, 23–27
  understanding, 10–11
  websites/software for help, 89
Debt calculators, 6
Debt management program (DMP), 49
Debtors Anonymous, 49, 160
Debt repayment worksheet, 11
Disposable income, 3, 6, 18

Edmunds car buying guides, 107
E-Loan, 123
Emergency funds, 159
Epstein, Lita, 149
Equifax Information Service Center, 29
Estate plan, 148–49
Estate Planning Basics (Clifford), 149
Estate Planning for Dummies (Simon
  and Caverly), 149
Experian Consumer Assistance, 29

Fair Isaac Corporation (FICO) score, 28,
  123
Family, enlisting cooperation of, 20–21,
  38–39
Financial independence, 151–57
Financial plan, 145–50
Financial planners, 13–14, 147–48
Food, savings on, 42–43
Foreclosure, 26–27, 68, 118
  401(k) plans, 87, 119, 138, 141, 142

Health maintenance organizations
  (HMOs), 129–30
Home(s). See also Mortgages

buying, 116–24
deductions for improvements, 94
investment value of, 116–17, 153
selling, 45, 63–64, 67
Home-based businesses, 114–15
Home equity, 63–68
  debt consolidation and, 33–34
  retirement and, 68, 136, 140
Home equity lines of credit, 33
Home equity loans, 33, 65, 66–67, 68, 86
Home refinancing, 27, 33, 34, 40–41
HomeShark, 123
Home warranties, 120

Income plan, 146
Inflation, 14, 116
Insurance, 125–33
  car, 26, 61, 111–12, 128–29
  credit, 132
  deductibles, 61, 131, 133
  dental, 132–33
  disability, 129
  for financial emergencies, 159–60
  flood, 131–32
  health, 129–31, 135–36
  homeowners, 61, 118, 131
  life (see Life insurance)
  mortgage, 41, 119
  provider for multiple policies, 133
  reducing premiums, 61, 111–12, 127–28,
    131
Interest rates
  compound, 102
  consolidating debts and, 32, 86, 88–89
  credit card, 11, 76–77, 87
  fixed, 11
  on home equity loans, 65
  on loans, 7, 24–25, 81
  paying off debts with high, 35
  reducing, 43, 47, 87
  on savings, 101
  variable, 11
Internet
  investment shopping on, 156
  mortgage shopping on, 123–24

Investments, 153–57
IRAs
Education, 70
Roth, 138, 139, 141, 142
self-directed, 139
traditional, 138–39, 142

Job, quitting, 114

Kelley Blue Book, 47, 59–60, 108, 109
Keough plans, 138
Kraemer, Sandy F., 149

Late payment fees, 25
Leaseback arrangements, 64
Life insurance, 126–28
cash value in, 86
term vs. whole life, 126, 127–28
Living wills, 148–49
Loans
adjustable-rate, 11
alternatives to short-term high-rate, 85
bad, 24–25, 80–85
car (see Car loans)
cause of high rates on, 7
credit union, 107
direct deposit advances, 82
equity line of credit, 60, 81
figuring costs of, 25
good, 80
home equity (see Home equity lines of
credit; Home equity loans)
inappropriate use of, 5–6, 23
installment, 11, 81
pawn shop, 82
payday, 82
questions to ask about, 82–83
refund anticipation, 26
retirement account, 83–84
revolving credit, 10, 81
secured, 8
three basic types, 81
unsecured, 8, 87

Medicare, 135, 137

Money
making more, 13, 113–15
searching for hidden, 57–62
Money.cnn.com, 152
Money magazine, 37, 62, 152, 153
Money market funds (MMFs), 100–101,
157
Moonlighting, 113–15
Morningstar Guide to Mutual Funds
(Benz), 156
Mortgages, 8, 11, 80
advantages of paying off, 88–89
affordable, 117
FICO score and, 123
fifteen- vs. thirty-year, 87–88
fixed- vs. variable-rate, 122
Internet shopping for, 123–24
reducing payments without refinancing,
41
reverse, 64
MSN Real Estate, 118, 124
Mutual funds, 155–56

New Car Buying Guide, 110
The 9 Steps to Financial Freedom
(Orman), 152

Orman, Suze, 152

Pagliarini, Robert, 152
Passbook savings accounts, 99
Paying yourself first, 53–56, 98
Pell Grants, 71
Perkins loans, 71
Preferred provider organizations (PPOs),
130
Prepayment penalties, 25, 35, 83
Prescription drug costs, 130–31, 137
Prime rate, 122
Progressive Insurance, 112

Quicken, 9, 89, 112, 124, 150

Renting a home, 42, 45, 118–19, 121
Rent-to-own deals, 25

Retirement, 14, 134–42
  amount needed to live on, 136
  change in expenses during, 137
  greatest fears about, 135
  home equity and, 68, 136, 140
  important issues to consider, 135–36
  loans against accounts, 83–84
  ordering finances for, 141–42
  readiness and affordability, 134–35
  sources for preparing for, 137
  tax-sheltered plans, 137–38
Retirement plan (financial plan section),
  146
Rye, David, 73, 137

Savings, 97–102
  budgeting for, 18
  compound interest on, 102
  finding money for, 97–98
  finding motivation for, 98
  five painless ways to start, 99
  getting started, 46–47
  good strategy for, 101–2
  home equity as, 66
  insufficiency of, 3, 5, 99–100
  interest rates on, 101
  from payments to yourself, 54–55
  recommended amount for, 98–99
Savings plan (financial plan section), 146
Scams, 35
Schwab, Charles, 137
Security plan, 146
SEP, 138
Simon, Jordan S., 149
The Six-Day Financial Makeover (Pagliarini), 152
60-Minute Estate Planner (Kraemer), 149
Small Business Catalog, 114
Social Security, 140–41
Spending
  excessive, 3–4, 5–6
  steps to reduce, 12, 24, 37–43
Spending plan, 4, 8–9, 17–18, 146
Stafford loans, 70–71
Student loans

  payments on, 59
  preferred, 70–71
Supplemental Education Opportunity
  Grants, 71

Taxes, 90–96
  Alternative Minimum, 91
  bracket, 90–91
  capital gains, 94, 140
  college expenses and, 70
  deductions, 11, 34, 64, 65, 66, 92, 94
  fear of the IRS, 93
  penalties, 84
  planning for, 93–94
  professional preparation of, 94–96
  property, 96, 118
  reducing withholding, 54, 91
  refunds, 54, 91, 99
  retirement plan shelters, 137–38
  saving receipts for, 92
  on social security income, 140–41
  storing records, 92–93
Taxpayer Relief Act of 1997, 70
Tax plan (financial plan section), 146
Trans Union Corp., 29
The 250 Estate Planning Questions
  Everyone Should Ask (Epstein), 149
The 250 Questions You Should Ask
  Before You Retire (Rye), 137

Used vs. new items, 58–59
Utility bills, reducing, 40

Wills, 148, 149–50

ABOUT THE AUTHORS

David Rye's career in personal coaching has convinced him that everyone would like to enhance his or her financial situation by getting out of debt. He was a director at IBM and taught personal finance at the University of Colorado. He elected to become president of Western Publications in 2000 so that he and his wife, Marcia, could devote all of their energies toward the subject of personal finance. The Ryes have written several personal finance books including *Two for the Money*, *The 250 Retirement Questions Everyone Should Ask*, and *1,001 Ways to Save, Grow, and Invest Your Money*.